INTERNATIONAL EDUCATION SERIES

FROEBEL'S EDUCATIONAL LAWS FOR ALL TEACHERS

INTERNATIONAL EDUCATION SERIES

FROEBEL'S EDUCATIONAL LAWS FOR ALL TEACHERS

by

JAMES L. HUGHES
INSPECTOR OF SCHOOLS, TORONTO

GYAN

Published by

GYAN

Gyan Publishing House
5, Ansari Road
Daryaganj, New Delhi-110002
Phone: 011-47034999, 9811692060
E-mail: books@gyanbooks.com

Distribution Network
gyanbooks.com
India, USA, Canada, UK, Australia, France

ISBN : 978-81-212-2301-0 (PB)
First Published, 1903

2nd Impression 2021

Printed at: Gyan Press, Delhi.

Froebel's Educational Laws for All Teachers
Author: James L. Hughes

INTERNATIONAL EDUCATION SERIES

FROEBEL'S EDUCATIONAL LAWS FOR ALL TEACHERS

BY

JAMES L. HUGHES

INSPECTOR OF SCHOOLS, TORONTO

"By and by Froebel's educational law will be accepted as distinctly and independently as Newton's law of gravitation."

BARONESS VON MARENHOLZ-BULOW

NEW YORK

D. APPLETON AND COMPANY

1903

EDITOR'S PREFACE.

The life of Friedrich Froebel falls in the time of the great German movement in philosophy. The birth year coincides very closely with the publication of the epoch-making book of Immanuel Kant—The Critique of Pure Reason. Kant had broken new ground for philosophy. He was followed by three giants, Fichte, Schelling, and Hegel, who continued his work and applied his results to the great problems of philosophy, namely, to the questions that relate to freedom, immortality, and the Divine Being. Kant uprooted, or supposed that he had uprooted, the old philosophy which had come down from Plato and Aristotle through the schoolmen of the Church. He thought that he had discovered a sound foundation for a new philosophy which could set at rest at least negatively the ultimate problems of life. Before his death, in 1804, he had seen applications of his new principle, first by Fichte, and afterward by Schelling—applications of which he had not had the slightest foreboding. What seemed an entirely new view of the world was projected by Fichte and Schelling. In the nature philosophy of the latter, time and space, matter and motion, gravitation and light, magnetism and crystallization, plant life and animal life, were "construed," to use his technical expression, as progressive realizations of mind in the objective pole of the being of the Absolute, mind being the subjective pole. All objects in nature containing positive and negative phases—like the magnet or electricity, or like chemical opposites—took on an interest for the thinker: they were lower orders of realization or far-off images of the Divine, which was supposed to have the form of mind and also to be the union of mind and Nature. Just as a magnet has north and south poles and an indifference point, so the Absolute is mind (as the subjective pole) and nature (as the objective pole), and it is also the union or indifference point of these two.

Just about the time of Kant's death (in 1804) Schelling began to change his view as to the nature of the Absolute as the indifference point of the two poles of ideality and reality. He began to draw the conclusion from his premises that the Absolute is not mind but the indifference point between mind and matter. It was at this juncture that Hegel, who had hitherto been his disciple, took final leave of his system. Hegel conceived the Absolute as a divine reason, and nature to him seemed to be the process by which the Divine Reason eternally creates infinitely manifold new individuals.

Froebel in the meantime had become fascinated with Schelling's first system, and he, too, like Hegel, adhered to the doctrine that the Absolute is mind. In his Education of Man, published in 1826, he expresses this doctrine in the following oft-quoted words: "In all things there lives and reigns an eternal law. This all-controlling law implies as its source an all-pervading, energizing, self-conscious, and hence eternal unity. This unity is God. From God all things have proceeded and they have their unity in the Divine Unity, in God alone. The divine effluence that lives in each thing is the essence of each thing. It is the destiny and life work of all things to unfold their essence, or their divine being, and therefore the Divine Unity itself—to reveal God in their external and transient being." Hence Froebel interpreted the special destiny and life work of man "to become fully, vividly, and clearly conscious of his essence, of the divine effluence in him, and therefore of God; to become fully, vividly, and clearly conscious of his destiny and life work; and to accomplish this, to render it (his essence) active, to reveal it in his own life with self-determination and freedom."

While Schelling laid great stress on art and literature, inasmuch as the æsthetic unity of mind and matter seemed to him to reach its highest point in sculpture, painting, music, and poetry, Froebel, in this respect, clings closer to the doctrines of Fichte, which make the striving of the human will to realize the good of far more importance than the creation of the beautiful. This accounts for the great stress which Froebel lays upon natural objects as the symbols of the mind. He does much to construct a scale of symbolic terms up which the mind of the child shall mount on its way to clear thinking. All of the categories of pure thought are used in the mind of the child, but not in their purity—they are incarnated or embodied in symbols or mental pictures, and it is the function of the sciences of arithmetic, geometry, grammar and logic, ethics and philosophy, to strip off the sensuous form in which these deep ideas first appear in the mind of the child, and give him ability to use them as tools of thought.

The kindergarten as it comes from the hands of Froebel is perhaps the most valuable educational method yet devised for giving the child the first impulse toward clearness of thinking and willing. As a bundle of feelings he is not yet clear either in his intellect or his will. One side of his feelings points toward the intellect and the other side points toward the will. The former is feeling in the form of sense-perception, the latter is in the form of desires, passions, and emotions. When the child translates his sensations into a knowledge of things and events he comes to his intellect. When he stands between his desires and his action and guides it, he attains to will and is a moral being.

I have used the word "symbolic" to describe the stage of mind in which the child finds himself at four years of age—to describe the frame of mind which feels the identity of nature and mind; it is a *growing* identity rather than a *realized* identity, and in the stage of feeling the child is supposed to have intimations of this profound unity between himself and the unconscious objects of nature amid which he finds himself. I admit that the word "symbol" is oftenest used in a narrower sense than this and signifies the employment of a natural object to convey a spiritual meaning. The philosophy of Froebel sees that all objects contain a kernel of spiritual meaning, and that it is impossible to think any phase of nature without at the same time bringing into the background of thought that spiritual idea.

W. T. Harris.

Washington, D. C., *January 12, 1897.*

PREFACE.

MANY teachers have failed to investigate the educational principles of Froebel because they believe that the founding of the kindergarten was Froebel's only educational work, and that the methods of the kindergarten are not adapted to the schoolroom. Both these opinions are incorrect. The principles upon which the kindergarten processes are based are fundamental principles that should guide the teacher in the work of teaching and training the child throughout its school course.

The veteran educator of England, Mr. J. G. Fitch, in his able report on training schools, made to the Education Department of England at the close of his long and honourable career, in speaking of the great advance recently made in the primary education of England and Wales, says:

"In watching the gradual development of the training colleges for women from year to year, nothing is more striking than the increased attention which is being paid in those institutions to the true principles of infant teaching and discipline. The circular which has recently been issued by your lordships, and which is designed to enforce and explain these principles, would, if put forth a few years ago, have fallen on unprepared soil, and would indeed have seemed to many teachers both in and out of training colleges to be scarcely intelligible. Now its counsels will be welcomed with sympathy and full appreciation. In almost every college a special course of lectures is provided on the teaching of Froebel and Pestalozzi, and on the application of their doctrines to the work of the infant school. Whatever is true and wise in the Froebelian and Pestalozzian philosophy is, in fact, applicable to all classes of children of all ages. Attempts to treat the kindergarten as a separate institution, having aims and methods of its own different from those which should prevail in other schools, have often in America and in Germany proved unsuccessful. It is as an organic part of a complete scheme of juvenile instruction, as a preliminary training of those faculties and aptitudes which have afterward to be developed when the time for serious application arrives, that the kindergarten is most valuable."

The kindergarten was Froebel's greatest work, but not his only educational work. The Education of Man was published in 1826, fourteen years before he opened his first kindergarten, yet if he had died in 1827, his contributions to educational thought would have given him a foremost place among educational reformers.

H. Courthope Bowen, in his admirable work on Froebel and Education through Self-Activity, says: "Froebel was possessed of large and generous views on education as a whole, and on its methods and results as wholes; but it is the work which he did for the education of infants between the ages of three and seven that chiefly demands our gratitude, so far as his aims have been realized up to the present; in the future, unless I am seriously mistaken, his *greatest service* will be in the reforms which his principles and methods will have forced on our *schools and colleges.*" And again: "It argues, therefore, an absolute misunderstanding of the whole matter to callously and indifferently admit that Froebel's ideas are true enough for the kindergarten, and at the same time to deny that they have anything to do with the school."

Dr. W. T. Harris, in the preface to The Education of Man, says: "Those who persistently read his works are always growing in insight and in power of higher achievement." This is the best influence one human being can have on another.

Froebel's work was to relate grand ideals to each other and to co-ordinate the theoretical and the practical. He transformed abstract principles into realities with consummate skill, and systematized the use of material things as agencies in the spiritual growth of the child to a degree never dreamed of by even the greatest educators who preceded him. He made valuable discoveries in education, but his grandest work was the crystallization of true ideals into a system. By doing so he made it possible for all honest, unprejudiced teachers, not blinded by presumptuous ignorance, to see what had hitherto been revealed only to the few whose free minds had swept beyond the range of fettered thought. He reduced to organized objective form theoretical truths which would have remained incomprehensible to the vast majority of teachers if he had not made them realities in the kindergarten. He wrote very wisely, but his profound writings would not have disseminated truth as clearly in centuries as his system in practice has done in a few years.

The aim of this book is to give a simple exposition of the most important principles of Froebel's educational philosophy, and to make suggestions regarding the application of these principles to the work of the schoolroom in teaching and training.

It has been my good fortune to know the leading kindergartners of America, and to have seen the practical work of most of them. For more than twenty years by the study of their writings, by personal discussion, and by observing their admirable work, I have sought to acquire clear views in regard to Froebel's philosophy, and to apply it in the work of the public schools. To all of them my indebtedness is freely acknowledged.

It is but just that I should express specially my gratitude for inspiration received from Madame Kraus-Boelte, Miss Susan E. Blow, Dr. Harris, Mr. and Mrs. Hailman, and Mr. H. Courthope Bowen, of London, England. Nor would I forget in this connection the constant suggestiveness of my wife, Ada Marean Hughes.

The quotations from Froebel have been made from Hailman's translation of The Education of Man, Froebel's Autobiography, translated by Michaelis and Moore, and Reminiscences of Froebel, by Baroness von Marenholz-Bülow. It is hoped that the grouping of his thought under topical headings may be of service.

JAMES L. HUGHES.

TORONTO, *September, 1896.*

CONTENTS.

FROEBEL'S EDUCATIONAL LAWS.

CHAPTER I.

THE DISTINCTIVE CHARACTERISTICS OF FROEBEL'S SYSTEM.

As an introduction to the study of Froebel's system it is important to take a general view of the characteristics that distinguish him from other educators.

Child Study.—Froebel made the child the chief agent in its own development. The child was the central point of his study. One of his mottoes was: "In the children lies the seed corn of the future." He recognised the power and the value of the teacher, but he realized very clearly that the teacher's influence might be too great. He reverenced the individuality of the child too much to allow the teacher to overshadow it, or prevent its growth by restrictive domination or by neglecting to give it the most ample opportunities for self-development.

Other educators have studied the child to learn what the teacher can do for it, what instruction it should receive, when it should be taught certain subjects, and how these subjects should be taught. Froebel studied the child to help it in its self-education, to discover the order of its mental and moral awakening, and the way in which it becomes acquainted with its environment and enters into its social relationships, and claimed that all educational methods should be in harmony with the natural processes of the child's own evolution. He revealed the fact that education is a work of growth carried on *by* and *through* the child, and not merely for it.

Froebel valued the work of the teacher as highly as other educators, but he placed a higher estimate on the child's own work than any other writer. His system does not lessen the need for wise and cultured teachers, but demands thorough training and broad culture on the part of all who have the privilege of training childhood. He does not reduce the work of the teacher, but he makes a radical change in its character.

Froebel's study of the child that he might learn its own processes of self-revelation, self-development, and self-enrichment, mentally and morally, laid the foundation for the deep interest in child study now shown so universally by teachers. Child study of a definite kind conducted systematically for the purpose of learning how the race should be taught and trained is a modern study. The physiological psychology of childhood and the recording of its spontaneous manifestations have only recently begun to occupy the attention of a few advanced experimental psychologists, but there has been a sudden awakening, and there are already many evidences of a widespread interest in these departments of educational investigation. The interest was undoubtedly aroused more rapidly by the establishment of kindergartens. They became objective representations of the great truth that children may be aided in self-education by supplying them with material to stimulate their creative activity. They recognised the sacredness of the child's individuality. They elevated the child above the mere knowledge which it is intended to use. They made the child the chief agent in its own development. They aimed to deal with the divinity rather than the depravity of the child. They helped to make real Emerson's ideal that the child is the "sun of the world." They revealed the fact that the child may be educated for a time most effectively without books. This made teachers think as they never had done of the relative value of the child and knowledge, and showed objectively the great importance of studying the child most carefully at all stages of its growth, so that it might be guided in its education in harmony with the laws of its natural development.

Unity or Inner Connection.—Froebel's system is based on the underlying law of unity. He meant more by unity than any other writer, either before or since his time. He saw relationships and inner connection with marvellous clearness. He saw unity between man and his Creator, and taught that the chief end of education is to make that unity perfect, so that humanity may become conscious of the unity, and that its consciousness of unity with God may lead it to reverent and co-operative activity with him. He saw the unity between God, Nature, and man, and therefore taught that Nature was the best revealer of God to the child. He saw the unity in the processes of growth and evolution to higher form in the living organisms of Nature, and thus made natural history and botany studies of the highest moral value. He saw the unity of the inorganic world so thoroughly, and expounded it in such minute details, that his explanations sometimes appear fanciful, as in crystallography, for instance; but even when modern science refuses to accept the theories he framed it must recognise in him an advanced scientist for his time. One can not escape the conviction that, if he had been fortunate enough to have had the advantage of the scientific development since his death, he would have seen even more clearly the unity of all created things, organic and inorganic, and the universal law working through them.

He saw the unity between man as an individual and man as a race and thereby laid the broadest basis for social relationships in the family, the municipality, the state, and the organic unity of humanity. He saw the unity between man's physical, intellectual, and spiritual powers, and thus broadened the basis of educational thought and effort, and showed the influence of every conscious act in the formation of character. He saw the unity that should exist between man's receptive, reflective, and executive powers, and on this revelation of unity based radical educational reforms, which have made clear the fallacy of attempting to elevate the race by giving it more power to acquire knowledge, without at the same time and by the same processes giving it greater power to apply knowledge, and greater tendency to use it definitely for good purposes. He saw the unity or continuity between childhood, youth, and manhood, and therefore realized the impossibility of reaching the highest limit of culture and power in manhood unless the fullest appropriate development has been reached in the preceding culture epochs of childhood and youth. It was this revelation that led him to see the imperative necessity for the kindergarten in order that the basal work of education might be done in such a way as to prepare the child for its most complete growth in succeeding periods of development. He claimed that the child was usually weakened to such an extent when it came to school that it never regained its lost power or attained the maximum limit of knowledge or skill which would have been possible if its mind had been properly stimulated, stored, and exercised. The weakening of the child's power before the school period he attributed to both positive and negative causes. The child was unduly dominated by its seniors, who had till Froebel's time never studied it sufficiently to understand it and fully sympathize with it; and few children were placed in conditions which were calculated to stimulate and define their own creative self-activity, which he regarded as the essential element in physical, intellectual, and moral development. On the one hand the child's spontaneity was checked by unreasoning repression, and on the other it was dwarfed by lack of opportunity for proper exercise. Such conditions he believed to be a barrier to the highest progress of the race, and he founded the kindergarten in order that the period of mightiest and most unlimited nascent possibilities in the child's life might be fully and systematically occupied in awakening and defining the complete circle of its powers. He saw the vital unity between the different departments of learning, and therefore planned a logical system of correlation of studies. He saw the unity between the subjective and the objective, and therefore taught the true inner connection between the sense training of Pestalozzi and the real mental growth of the child. He understood the fundamental law of mind development by apperception as thoroughly as Herbart, and made his whole system contribute to the awakening of the inner power and experience of the child which is most directly related to the new experience or to the fresh presentation of knowledge. He saw the unity between knowing, feeling, and willing, between analysis and synthesis, between thought and life. He saw the unity or inner connection of all created things so clearly that he made the reconciliation of opposites an important element of his system. He believed this law of unity, inner connection, or vital interrelationship to be universal, and made it the fundamental law and the ultimate aim of all true educational effort.

Self-Activity.—As unity is Froebel's fundamental law, so self-activity is his essential educational process. His recognition and wonderful application of self-activity is the most comprehensive and the most distinctive element in his educational system. It is the most productive educational principle that has yet been discovered. It involves the doctrines of interest and apperception not merely as educational theories, but as applied educational principles called into play naturally and forcefully as essential steps in guiding and determining the activities of the child. It makes the child the centre upon which all true correlation is focused. It is the only process by which the co-ordination of the child's brain can be made complete. It makes the child an executive as well as a receptive and reflective being, and thereby overcomes the most universal human weakness of failing to live and act up to the limit of individual knowing and thinking. It reveals the child to its teacher and to itself by making the inner become the outer life. It defines the feeling and thought of the child and makes it original and progressive. It is the truest basis of self-faith and independence of character, without which the strongest and most cultured intellect is not adequately efficient as a productive or an uplifting force. It makes the child not only responsively, but also suggestively co-operative with its teachers and parents, so that it becomes a co-worker, not a follower, and a creative instead of an imitative agent.

Froebel's ideal of self-activity is distinctively his own. No writer before his time conceived the idea, and few writers since have thoroughly understood it. When it is grasped in its full meaning by educators it will remove more weaknesses and errors from the methods of teachers, and form the basis of greater reforms than any other educational principle. It must not be confounded with the activity of the child in performing operations in response to the command or suggestion of its teacher or any other person. It is the spontaneous effort of the child to make manifest to itself and others the inner conceptions and operations of its own mind. In true self-activity the motive or impulse that causes the action originates with the child itself. Other educators saw the necessity for training the child to act; Froebel saw that the child should be trained to act independently. Other educators aimed to develop power to perform certain operations; he gave power to direct operations in addition to the power to perform them. He trained the will to control the activities of the being. He developed tendency to do, wisdom in deciding what to do, and will to govern the doing, in connection with the operations that have been used by other educators to develop only skill in execution. Other educators gave the child power to do its part well under certain conditions; he not only gave this, but also the power to mould conditions, to see opportunities, and to choose those best suited to individual taste and ability. He increased spontaneity of will action and expertness in execution at the same time; other educators have aimed to develop them separately or have failed altogether to give attention to the former.

Early Training of Sensations and Emotions.—Froebel endeavoured to place the child in such conditions as to define its sensations and emotions, and prepared for mothers and kindergartners a very complete system of songs, games, and suggestions—The Mother Play—to guide them in stimulating and fostering the sensations and emotions of children. In writing about The Mother Play, he said: "This book is the starting point of a natural system of education for the first years of life, for it teaches the way in which the germs of human dispositions should be nourished and fostered if they are to attain to complete and healthy development." This book he regarded as the most important part of his educational work, because it dealt with a department of education which had been neglected by all other educators, and because he believed that the strength and the possible development of the mind in after life depend on the wideness of range and definiteness of the fundamental emotions and sensations. In one of the remarkable conversations with the Baroness von Marenholz-Bülow, he said: "The understanding of the unconscious is the germ and the beginning of the conscious, and so surely as they stand in connection with each other, so surely the one as well as the other has its origin in unity—"God." He not only realized that apperception was essential in the evolution of mind, he saw that apperception could not take place unless the mind contained the germ elements corresponding to the new knowledge to be communicated to it, and he wished to form apperceptive centres in the heart as well as in the mind. He valued apperceptive centres of feeling even more than apperceptive centres of thought. He reasoned that the more the child's sensations and emotions are defined and varied the greater its possibilities for growth become, and he wisely concluded that the worst period during the life of a human being in which to leave his mental and moral evolution to chance is the time when his mind and heart are being organized and charged with the power centres which to so large an extent decide his tendency, his range, and his strength. He planned a system of education that would give the child experience as a basis for instruction and for ethical culture, and demanded that the home and kindergarten should send a child to school with "a foundation, a basis, a sum of living germs in the life material it has gathered." In this department of educational investigation he had the widest scope for originality. No one had preceded him, and few have yet been able to follow where he led. There is still need of intelligent study on the part of educators to extend the good work begun by Froebel in order to increase the stock of germ elements in the minds and hearts of children before they go to school—even before they go the kindergarten. The need for this definite training of the child's powers of sensation and emotion in its earliest years has been greatly increased since Froebel's time by the extraordinary recent growth of great cities. Both in Europe and America the number and size of cities and large towns has rapidly increased. The tendency to leave the farm and the forest for the supposed advantages of urban life is one of the alarming social movements of the age. The children are the greatest losers by this change. The child brought up in the country close to the glories of Nature has the opportunity to obtain a much richer mental and moral foundation than the child who lives in the city. If allowed its freedom among the flowers, the trees, the birds, the insects, and the ever-changing growth of Nature in its varied forms of living and transforming or evolving organisms, the country child needs little guidance in gaining a wide experience of sensations and emotions as a basis for its future conscious development. Here the child needs but the perfect sympathy of its mother, in love with Nature and with her child, in order to have its mind filled with a vast store of the germs of mental strength and moral beauty, which are ever freely communicated to the child or the man who can hear what Nature is whispering or see what she is doing. In cities the child is not so fortunate. Its range is limited and the conditions are unnatural. Therefore, while The Mother Play is invaluable to all teachers, kindergartners, and mothers, it is needed especially in the homes of cities and towns to widen and define the experiences of children so that they may have minds full of germ centres to which the varied knowledge to be given in the schools may be clearly related, and hearts in which the emotional foundations of character have been laid.

Theory of Evolution.—The theory of evolution was not discovered by Froebel, but he first made it a definite element in a system of education. He did not recognise it merely as a philosophical educational theory, he made it a practical reality. One of his distinctive characteristics is his genius for reducing philosophical and psychological principles to definite pedagogical practice. This gives value to all his educational work. He gave to teachers concrete representations of educational theories. He made it impossible to carry out his system without practising the principles involved in it, and thus made the revelation of educational concepts to the minds of teachers conform to the law of "learning to do by doing." By his objective representation of educational principles in practical operation he made it possible for philosophic minds to recognise them better than he did himself. Many of the writers on evolution since his time have been indebted to him for their philosophy of evolution. Throughout The Education of Man, and, indeed, in all Froebel's works, all his thoughts, methods, systems, and processes are associated with the idea of a natural and a gradual evolution to higher degrees of development. He found evidences of this in individual plants and in plant life as a whole. He noted that care, culture, and full opportunity produced finer individual flowers, and that by the interfructification of the best specimens a higher type might be developed, in which even the characteristic structure might be improved. He found in Nature a continuity in the ascending stages from the lowest types of organized life through plant and animal life up to man himself. He saw that development in the individual and in the species is from within, and that exercise of function is the universal law underlying the increase of functional power. He saw that conditions and environment and nurture have a great influence on the character of the plant or animal, but he saw also that the dominant influence in the development of the plant or animal is its own inner life. He reasoned that all life is subject to the law of evolution, and that the higher the type of living organism the less the influence of material things must be in retarding or accelerating its development, and the greater the possibility of higher evolution. He planned, therefore, a definite system for the evolution of humanity through its successive periods of infancy, childhood, youth, and manhood, the foundations of which he concluded by analogy should be freedom, stimulating environment, ample opportunity, appropriate knowledge, and self-activity. He finished the details of the earliest period only, but he had planned a similar definite system for the higher departments of education. He believed that every age should reach a higher stage of culture and power than the preceding one, physically, intellectually, and spiritually. He hoped for new inventions to deal with material things, and grander intellectual and spiritual revelations with each successive era. He taught that education should be one of the most progressive departments of human thought and effort, and tried to lead each individual to believe that he had power to help humanity to climb, and that the unselfish use of this power was his highest duty and the source of his most perfect happiness. Thus he made evolution a self-adjusting, reproductive, progressive process, and education the application of this process in the development of humanity. His whole educational system was an earnest protest against the idea that education could be superimposed on the child from without. He said, in summing up the essential principles explained in The Education of Man: "God neither ingrafts nor inoculates. He develops the most trivial and imperfect things in continuously ascending series, and in accordance with eternal self-grounded and self-developing laws."

His educational law of evolution was based on his belief in the unity between divinity and humanity. He utterly discarded the doctrine of the total depravity of the child. He believed that even in the most depraved and uncultivated races and individuals there is an element of the divine, and that all true education is "a conscious growth toward the divine." He aimed to reveal God to the child as the unseen power in the natural forces and the natural life around it, in order that a conscious unity might be established between God and the element of divinity in man. This conscious unity he made the foundation of his faith in education as an evolutionary agency. The divinity in the child he regarded as its individuality, and therefore he demanded for true individuality the most sacred reverence and perfect freedom. He recognised very clearly the terrible evidences of deterioration and degeneracy in human nature through heredity, but he believed that while the evils brought into human nature may obscure the divinity in it, they can not eradicate it, and that when even the smallest element of divinity in the child is brought into activity in acordance with the Creator's law of evolution, it becomes an uplifting, self-developing, and reproductive force, that will gradually triumph over the evils of heredity. The very fact that he found different degrees of development in humanity, as he did in the vegetable and animal world, convinced him that those in the lower degrees must, under proper conditions, in conformity to a law which he conceived to be universal, advance to higher conditions, and that those in the highest could rise more rapidly to still higher degrees of development.

The application of the law of evolution to education has revolutionized the views of teachers in regard to the functions of education. Men and women are now investigating educational forces with the child as the dominant element. There is hope for the teacher in the widening conception of the possibilities of human evolution based on reverence for the child.

The unfolding of this law is leading to a logical settlement of all questions relating to the studies that should find a place in educational courses. These questions are not yet decided. The best for to-day may not be the best for all the coming days. The discussions are focused now on the child and the effectiveness of different kinds of knowledge as elements in producing the broadest, richest, strongest development appropriate to the successive and interrelated stages of its growth. Froebel's motto, "The renovation of life," is taking the place of the old ideal that "knowledge is power."

Individuality.—Froebel's conception of the sacredness of the child's individuality is one of the prominent characteristics of his system. He taught that every child has special power, and that its fullest growth and truest education can not be attained unless this special power becomes the dominant element in its life—the central current, to which all its other powers form tributary streams. He made this the guiding principle in his disciplinary agencies. The continued coercion of another being, parent or teacher, he regarded as a gross injustice certain to prevent the full development of the child. He condemned all disciplinary agencies which in any way overshadow the child or interfere with its sense of perfect freedom. Free growth is the only full growth.

He did not advocate giving the child unrestrained liberty to do wrong. He rejected the theory that children love to do wrong better than right, and regarded the transference of interest on the part of the child from wrong to right as the foundation on which true training is based. The power to transfer interest naturally from wrong to right is the greatest power of the parent or teacher in co-operating with the child in its own moral and intellectual culture. His theory rested on the following well-defined, related principles: The child's own self-activity must be the agency of its truest and fullest development. Self-activity is impossible under restraint. The child loves to do right better than to do wrong, to be constructive better than to be destructive. The well-trained teacher can change the centre of interest without coercion, and without interrupting the operation of self-activity. Therefore the child's selfhood may be sacredly respected without endangering its own moral nature or the rights of others. By the wise application of these principles he established the perfect harmony between control and spontaneity, and burst the fetters of external limitations to the soul.

The progress of the ages has been a growth toward freedom. The true ideal of freedom can never be conceived by a mind that has been made conscious of subjection to another mind. Subordination is an unmixed evil. Froebel stands pre-eminent among educators by his recognition of the child's individuality, and by the success he achieved in providing for its unrestricted development in his educational system.

Co-operation.—Froebel's recognition of individuality did not end in individualism. His universal law of inner connection or unity gave him power to see individual man in his relationship to the whole of humanity. He therefore aimed to make each man as perfect as possible in order that he might completely fulfil his duty as a part of the brotherhood of man, knowing that the character of the organized whole depends on the development of its individual elements. His prophet soul saw clearly what has even yet been revealed to few of the leaders of advanced sociology—that there is an essential unity existing beween individualism and socialism. When his educational principles have been practised long enough to make them dominant elements in human character there will be an end to the illogical socialism that demands compulsory co-operation in defiance of individual rights. His kindergarten or school was a little world where responsibility was shared by all, individual rights respected by all, brotherly sympathy developed in all, and voluntary co-operation practised by all. He denied that good citizenship can be produced by knowledge alone, however carefully it may be selected with respect to its own value and its adaptation to the stages of the child's development. He insisted that character is formed by living the principles of truth, justice, and freedom, and not by learning them. He believed that self-activity is even more essential in the organization of the varied powers of a being into the unity called character than it is in the development of the individual elements of power. So he made his school and his kindergarten conform as far as possible to the conditions of an ideal society in order to qualify the race for greater, truer, purer, more unselfish living in the wider spheres of social and national life. He did not claim that the positive and negative evils wrought into the sensitive organism of human nature by centuries of restrictive conditions can be eradicated or overcome completely in a single generation, but he did teach that it can be most effectively wrought out by performing unselfish, loving deeds, and that the true altruistic spirit springs from the recognition of the unity of society as the supreme element in deciding human relationships. This recognition of social unity, interrelationship, and duty, Froebel aimed to define in early childhood, not by theoretical instruction, but by making his kindergartens and schools essentially social organizations. He avoided the errors of the Grecian ideal of social unity which dwarfed individual development. He condemned national and social unity based on coercion, and made freedom the essential element in the highest culture of individuality, and the most perfect organization of society. His social theory was based on the belief that individual development can never be complete until it is stimulated to its fullest limit and highest effort by the inspiring consciousness of the intimate interrelationship of the individual members of society, and the consequent impelling possibilities of uplifting influence on humanity. This is the highest motive and it gives majesty to individual selfhood, because it frees it from all the narrowness and selfishness of exclusive individualism. Selfishness is always restrictive; socialism may dwarf individuality. Froebel saw the harmony between egoism and altruism, and saw in the indirect training of the properly organized school the hope of revealing this harmony to coming generations. When a few generations shall have passed through such schools teachers will fully comprehend Froebel's prophetic revelation of the unity between co-operation and perfect individuality, and the war between individualism and socialism shall be at an end.

Nature Study.—Froebel's idea in regard to Nature study was a revelation. He was a passionate student of the life principle in Nature. Even while serving as a soldier he collected new plants discovered during the tiresome marches of the day, in order that he might become acquainted with them by the camp fire in the evening. He reverenced plant life too much to destroy it unnecessarily. He preferred to make his observations of plants while they were growing. He saw in the growth and evolution of life in Nature types of the true growth and evolution of life toward higher life. He consequently regarded plant culture as a much higher and more productive study for the child than plant analysis and classification. He made Nature study and Nature nurture an important part of his educational system chiefly on account of its ethical influence. He believed that through the discovery of the life in natural things and by an early recognition of an unseen power in the forces of Nature, the child secured most easily and most thoroughly the germs of spiritual power and a true conception of God as the source of life. He taught the child to plant seeds and water them till they germinated, and then to care for the plants as they grew to maturity, in order to reveal its own power to aid in bringing into existence new life and to help to higher life the life that already exists. The child's action in developing the seed and the plant reveals, by the symbolism which Froebel recognised more clearly than any other educator, the possibilities of helpfulness and uplifting power which the individual man may exercise in the elevation of his fellow-men. He objected to formal lessons on duty, morality, and religion, because he believed it to be impossible to convey knowledge in regard to these great questions until their fundamental elements had entered the minds of children through experience. The laws that govern apperception in acquiring knowledge in other departments of culture apply with equal force in the sphere of ethics. To try to force moral and religious truth into the child's mind from the outside is certain to prevent true moral and religious growth, and substitute for it a self-deceptive formalism and a destructive hypocrisy.

He believed that through Nature the child could best get ideas appropriate to its stage of development, relating to beauty, purity, growth, evolution to higher life, the consciousness of an unseen power, of life in life and life behind life, of God, and of co-operation with the unseen life—God. He believed that without a basis of such germ thoughts and feelings the great principles of religious faith and life could never become vital elements in the life of a human soul.

Nature study was therefore to Froebel not only the best preparation for botany and zoölogy, and the centre of educational effort around which he would correlate all other studies, but the basis of definite and thorough ethical training.

Objective Work.—Froebel's use of material is destined to revolutionize the methods of object teaching. Pestalozzi gave a mighty impulse to objective work in schools. Unfortunately his aim was misunderstood by nearly all the English and American educators of his time. He made his pupils examine and handle real things for the purpose of giving a definite training to their powers of acquiring knowledge, but English and American teachers adopted his objective work as a means of giving knowledge to their pupils more easily and more clearly. Nearly all the books on object teaching yet published in English perpetuate this error. They are mainly guides in conducting information lessons, which reveal no trace of Pestalozzi's aim. The English Education Department wisely eliminated object lessons from the English Code in 1861, and continued the proscription for twenty years, till the principles of Pestalozzi and Froebel were better understood. Pestalozzi's aim is now more widely understood both in England and America, although there is still a large amount of "object-lesson" work of a character inferior to that done by the great founder of the method. Froebel gave material to the child to arouse and develop its creative faculties and to provide varied and definite experiences for it. The highest use that can be made of material is to make it the basis of the enlargement of the mind and the development of originality. Froebel used it for these purposes. His aim was not mind storing, nor the increase of strength in the receptive powers of the mind. He recognised the need of mind storing and faculty training, but he saw that he could secure these advantages most definitely and most naturally by making them essential processes in a wider, higher ideal. Creative self-activity was Froebel's inclusive ideal. All subordinate ideals are bounded by limitations of interest. Mind storing as mind storing loses its charm, faculty training as faculty training ceases to have arousing power, unless it is related to some greater design. Creative self-activity is at once the most natural, the most comprehensive, and the most stimulating mental occupation. Having realized this as Froebel did with great clearness, he used objects not merely for investigation but for rearrangement, readjustment, and reconstruction in order to represent and express the conceptions and designs of the child itself. He accomplishes mind storing and faculty training more thoroughly than Pestalozzi, and at the same time he uses material things as agencies for self-revelation and self-expression. Many teachers have used objects to promote learning. Pestalozzi asked, What powers can I define and develop by objects? Froebel said: I shall lead the child to express his own conceptions with real things. Learning, defining, doing, are the three steps in his evolutionary sequence. The third includes the other two.

Manual Training.—Froebel was the founder of the rational system of manual training. The world did not at first understand his views in regard to manual training. The most advanced schools have yet barely reached his advanced ideals. The utilitarian aspect of manual training has dwarfed the conceptions of educators until recent years in studying the subject. This view did not influence Froebel. He knew that what is philosophically true must be at the same time most practical. He placed manual training on an educational instead of an economic or industrial basis. He made the hand the chief agent in developing the mind. The use of material things to represent or express the original conceptions of the child affords the best possible opportunities for developing the child's creative power and executive ability, for co-ordinating its brain, and for revealing to it the fact that it has power to mould and use the material world around it. For all these ideals in regard to manual training we are indebted to Froebel. He valued the inner results of manual training in the child more than the outer material products.

All the advancement made in educational thought concerning manual training has been made toward Froebel's views, and he is still the leader. From trade schools, which were as far as possible from Froebel's ideal, teachers have slowly passed through the stages of using manual training for economic purposes, till at length the most progressive have grasped his conception—that manual training is thought expression, and an important process in the child's mental and moral development.

Froebel differed radically from his successors in regard to the period of the child's life when manual training is of greatest educational value. Blinded by the industrial ideal, they gave manual training only to the highest classes, and therefore necessarily to comparatively few. He prepared a system adapted to the youngest children, and for all children, girls as well as boys. Here, too, the modern leaders have their faces turned toward Froebel.

Very few have yet caught a glimpse of Froebel's highest thought about manual training. He made it the operative basis of spiritual evolution. The revelation of the creative power of humanity is the surest basis for the progressive achievement of unity between humanity and God. By manual training the boy is planting in his own nature the germs of the vital thought that he has power "to give body to spirit and form to thought."

The Educational Value of Play.—While Froebel was not the first to see the educational value of play, he was the first to make play an essential part of school work. Many educators—Plato, Quintilian, Fenélon, Locke, Richter, and others—had recognised the educational importance of play, and had written wisely about the subject. A great wave of interest in play as a factor in the physical development of the race swept over Germany during the life of Froebel. It was started by Gutsmuths in 1796 and has continued to increase in power for a century. More books were written on this subject in Germany during the past century than have been written about play in all other countries since the world began. This remarkable interest culminated in the establishment of public playgrounds throughout

Germany nearly a century after Gutsmuths began his agitation. These playgrounds are not for mere physical exercise. They are supervised by competent men who have received some training in psychology, and who are therefore able to understand the relation of play to human growth.

It was perfectly natural that Froebel should be influenced by the great play movement of his time, and, having his interest aroused, he, as was usual with him, at once proceeded to turn his theories into definite educational methods. His extraordinary insight into the law of inner connection enabled him to see the intellectual and moral advantages of play as well as its physical benefits, and in his system play became an important element in the complete development of the child. He utilized the instinctive tendency to play as a factor in the training of the child without robbing the play of its essential element of spontaneity.

The Harmony between Spontaneity and Control.—Froebel's educational reforms have been grasped more generally in the department of discipline than in any other department of school work. Yet, even here he is only partially understood. The feeling that underlies his work has spread much more rapidly than his thought, but the practice of a more natural and more humane discipline is making the revelation of his thought more complete.

His recognition of the sacredness of the child's individuality was so clear that restriction, coercion, and the domination of the teacher were at once removed from the list of his disciplinary agencies. Restriction dwarfs, coercion blights, and domination destroys individuality, and therefore Froebel waged against them a war of extermination. He refused to destroy power and character in the effort to educate.

His comprehension of the interrelationships existing between all the truly developing processes of Nature made him decide that, even between essential freedom and desirable control, there must be a mediate course that produces perfect harmony, so he sought the "perfect law of liberty" that he might guide childhood without destroying its spontaneity.

He believed so thoroughly in the law of evolutionary development through successive stages of human growth that he did not expect finished character in a child. He was satisfied to allow to little children a condition of liberty which shocked the martinets, and shocks some of them still. He denied that anarchy is caused by freedom, but asserted strongly that it is the natural result of enforced control, and that unnatural control, especially during unconscious childhood, makes the child conscious in a weakening sense, and leads to indifference or resistance to constituted authority.

He found self-activity to be the intermediary process to produce harmony between spontaneity and control, and interest to be the motive that leads to self-activity when the selfhood has not been made passive by arbitrary control. With loving sympathy as an attractive power, making the teacher a friend instead of a domineering autocrat, and with the interested self-activity of the child as the central thought in the teacher's philosophy, he knew discipline would settle itself in a natural way. He refused to believe that children are happier when they are doing wrong than when doing right, and never for a moment doubted that they are happier when engaged in appropriate occupations than when idle.

Starting with these foundation principles, he concluded that the true inner life of the child can be made to grow, as the inner life of any other living organism grows, by placing it in proper conditions. The teacher's duty is like the gardener's—to supply the desirable conditions. The natural conditions of child growth he believed to be love, joyousness, and interested occupation—mainly self-activity. He insisted that when a child is supplied with these conditions it is unnatural for it to misbehave if its health is good. Productivity being, according to his philosophy, the true function of humanity, he reasoned that creative self-activity is the most perfect source of human happiness, and the only rational agency in truly developing discipline.

"But all children do not like to work," answers the objector. Better say, "All children do not like to do the work you choose for them." That is likely to be very true. The wonder is that any of them like work chosen for them by others, and to which they are driven by the authority of the teacher. Even when the persuasive power is the witchery of loving reverence for the teacher, work chosen by another never has the maximum of power to interest or develop, and can not long hold the attention of the pupil or make the path of duty the path of pleasure. Froebel had no doubt of the love of the children for productive work if they were trained to plan work as well as perform it. "They yield themselves," said he, "in childlike trust and cheerfulness to their formative and creative instinct."

During the early unconscious period of the child's development Froebel would have the control of the mother and kindergartner so thoroughly in harmony with the spontaneity of the child as not to be felt by it. The highest disciplinary skill of the mother or kindergartner is shown by the transference of the child's interest from evil to good in so natural a way that the child is not conscious of the external guiding influence in making the change or of its own surrender of one interest for another. To be conscious of the direct influence would make it a follower instead of an independent agent.

When the child becomes conscious of its own personality the teacher's duty is still to maintain the harmony between control and spontaneity. Now, however, both the control and the spontaneity should belong to the pupil. The control should become self-control, and this should be developed, first, by a clear recognition of the rights of others, and, second, by a realization of the personal advantages resulting from self-control in subordinating the undesirable to the desirable in one's own tendencies. During this period the teacher should be the confidential friend of the pupil, and not a mere dictator to whom the pupil should render unquestioning obedience. Exigencies may arise when the teacher may wisely say 'Thou shalt" or "Thou shalt not," as the result of the "better choice between two evils." Such an incident is always a moral catastrophe, and the wise teacher undoes the evil so far as possible when the conditions that precipitated the collision have passed away. During the reaction in the child's nature after such an unfortunate collision it is often possible for the loving heart of the teacher to find a widened entrance to the heart of the pupil. Such collisions are most disastrous when rebellion is aroused by dictatorial authority.

Froebel's idea of a unity or harmony between control and spontaneity is worthy of most careful study. When it is fully understood the discipline of all schools will be placed on a new basis, and discipline will become what it should be—a most important agency in the formation of character.

Women as Teachers.—Froebel made a radical reform in educational work by his recognition of woman as the proper educator of childhood. Pestalozzi had pleaded for a motherhood of culture and sympathy. Herder had said to women: "Meditate upon and educate (for you alone can do it) a happy posterity." Froebel did much more than plead with mothers. He planned a systematic course of training for them to give to their children. With his usual habit of transforming insight into attainment, he first saw that "the destiny of nations lies far more in the hands of women—the mothers—than in the possessors of power," and he then made practical plans to qualify women for their work and guide them in it. A favourite motto of his, which he frequently emphasized, was: "We must educate women, who are the educators of the race, else the new generation can not accomplish its task." He said to the Baroness von Marenholz-Bülow: "Women are my natural allies, and they ought to help me, for I bring to them what shall relieve them of their inner and outer fetters, terminate their tutelage, and restore their dignity with that of still undervalued childhood." He repeated the same views to Herr von Wydenbrugk: "Women and children are the most oppressed and neglected of all. They have not yet been fully recognised in their dignity as parts of human society. If progress and a greater degree of freedom depend largely upon the degree of universal culture, then it is woman to whom God and Nature have pointed out the first educational office in the family, upon whom this progress especially depends." In conversation with his dear friend Middendorff, he said: "Women are to recognise that childhood and womanliness (the care of childhood and the life of women) are inseparably connected, that they form a unit, and that God and Nature have placed the protection of the human plant in their hands. The culture of individuals, and therefore of the whole nation, depends in great part on the earliest care of childhood. On that account women, as one half of mankind, have to undertake the most important part of the problems of the time—problems that men are not able to solve. If but one half of the work be accomplished, then our epoch, like all others, will fail to reach the appointed goal. As educators of mankind, the women of the present time have the highest duty to perform, while hitherto they have been scarcely more than the beloved mothers of human beings."

"Tell women to take part immediately by their educational activity in the destiny of nations; tell them that the recognition of the dignity of the female sex depends upon this. The sex must be torn not only from its instinctive and passive, but from its merely personal life, in order to live as a conscious member of humanity. The consciousness of its elevated life work, and the capacity truly to accomplish it, will do more to bring on the kingdom of God than all other means."

His Mother Play was prepared for mothers that they might lay in infancy the only sure foundations for intellectual and moral growth by defining the sensations, directing the emotions, and extending the experiences of their children. He hoped to have this book intelligently studied by mothers everywhere. The great movement now going on in Europe and America in favour of the establishment of mothers' classes and clubs for the study of The Mother Play gives hope that his plan may soon be realized.

The greatest step made toward the full recognition of woman's individuality and responsibility since the time of Christ was made when Froebel founded his kindergartens and made women educators outside the home—educators by profession. This momentous reform gave the first great impetus to the movement in favour of woman's freedom and provided for the general advance of humanity to a higher plane by giving childhood more considerate, more sympathetic, and more stimulating teachers.

Symbolism.—One of Froebel's strongest claims to the title of the "psychologist of childhood" is his remarkable insight into the power of children to recognise analogies and resemblances, to clothe even inanimate things with life, to give personality to everything, to see hidden meanings and relationships—in short, to see spiritual associations. This led him to give symbolism so prominent a place in his system, and this element in his educational work distinguishes him as much as any other principle from the educators who preceded him as well as from most of his successors. By trying to remember the spiritual insights of their own earliest years and by carefully watching the manifestations of the dawning associations in the minds of very young children, many teachers and educational investigators are beginning to realize the importance of idealizing or spiritualizing things, actions, and stories for the little ones as a part in their highest education—spiritual education. No one doubts that the spiritual nature is capable of more limitless development than either the physical or the intellectual. It is impossible to overestimate the good influence of a complete spiritual development on the culture of the other departments of our natures or the loss to humanity at large resulting from the failure to give definite training to the spiritual powers. We pass through life almost in touch with momentous spiritual problems that are never revealed to us because our spiritual insight has not been developed, or has been weakened by neglect. Froebel's recognition of the law of continuity showed him the importance of laying the basis for future growth in early childhood. He was especially anxious to develop spiritual insight in the discovery of analogies, so as to prepare for the revelation of universal unity in manhood. This he believed to be the great purpose of education. This gives the highest reason for the cultivation of the imagination.

Miss Blow, in her profoundly philosophic work on Symbolic Education, summarizes Froebel's symbolism in the kindergarten as "an endeavour through the use of typical facts and poetic analogies to stir the child with far-away presentiments of his ideal nature, his spiritual relationships, and his divine destiny." In the planning of his whole kindergarten system of gifts, occupations, plays, games, and stories he kept in view the cultivation of the power to discover analogies. The individual gifts themselves and the manifold things they are made to form or represent are used by the children to typify the varied visions of a child's imagination. The continuity insisted upon by Froebel in the use of the gifts by evolving one structure or article or form from another without resolving the first into its constituent elements and the perfect rational sequence existing among the gifts themselves were intended to foreshadow in the mind of the child the related continuity between the stages of the life of man. In the plays and games every relationship of the child to its home, society, Nature, and God are exemplified; the occupations and some of the games prepare the child for the comprehension in later life of the interdependence of all grades of society, and lay the foundation of the reverence that one class should have for the honest workers in all other fields of effort; and a still higher kind of symbolism is found in the games that illustrate spiritual truths and ethical principles. His stories, too, are used in a similar way to fill the child's mind and spiritual nature with the germ-structures around which its spiritual insights and ethical character may establish themselves.

The interpretation of the spiritual through the real is a definite stage in spiritual evolution. It is quite as essential to have apperceptive centres for spiritual growth as for intellectual development and the assimilation of knowledge. By placing the child in proper conditions, bringing it in contact with Nature, directing its activities in lines that will reveal unity, evolution, and logical sequence, it is possible to foreshadow during the child's unconscious period the deepest mysteries of its intellectual and spiritual life. Froebel's greatest work, The Mother Play, is worthy of careful study not only by mothers and kindergartners, but by all teachers, as a philosophical foundation for the complete intellectual and spiritual awakening and evolution of childhood.

Froebel gave a needed lesson to all teachers in public schools and in Sunday schools by his instructions, that the inner symbolism of the child's work or play should not be brought specifically into the child's consciousness by any formal explanations or moralising by the teacher or kindergartner. Evil always results from adult interference with the natural evolution of unconsciousness into consciousness. Symbolism is in harmony with child nature, and in due time the foreshadowed spiritual ideals will reveal themselves in the child's mind and life. The function of adult wisdom is to provide the conditions for implanting the symbolic germs of vital principles in the mind of unconscious childhood. The unfolding of the germs into controlling principles should be the work of later years. The habit of "pointing the moral" of tale or incident is a kindred error to the practice of forcing mature theories of religion or adult practices of the child. Miss Blow admirably expresses this idea in the sentence: "Froebel knows that the mind may be trusted to universalize its ideas, and leaves to its own alchemy the transmutation of the symbol into the reality symbolized."

Froebel wrote comparatively little under the title "Symbolism," but he made it an element in all his early education. What he said is sufficient to show how much importance he attached to it:

"Childhood can only be led through symbols to the understanding of truth and the understanding of itself. It needs symbolic action."

"The presentiment of truth always goes before recognition of it."

"I have not only forms for the child's eyes, which are to make him acquainted with the outer world which surrounds him; I have symbols which unlock his soul for the thought or spirit which is innate in everything that has come out of God's creative mind. If the ripened mind is to know and understand this thought, its embodied image must make an impression upon the yet unconscious soul of the child, and leave behind it forms which can serve as analogies to the intellectual ordering of things."

Some attempts have been made, especially in Sunday schools, to create an unnatural, conventional symbolism by establishing a code of material symbols to represent spiritual ideals. It is an error that violates every fundamental principle of evolution and self-activity to try to fit adult ideas of symbolism to the child's mind.

The Comprehensiveness of Froebel's Philosophy.—Those who have been disposed to regard Froebel as a mere enthusiast guided chiefly by his feelings should be led to a due appreciation of his greatness by the fact that he first clearly recognised several great truths which since he revealed them have become the central elements in the writings of the most philosophical industrial, social, and moral reformers.

Dr. Stanley Hall says: "Froebel's philosophy of education is to me, on the whole, the best we have, in that it brings out more elements and gives them a truer proportion. The root and spirit of Christianity are in it; so is the spirit of Bacon and Comenius; so is the chief *motif* of the German idealistic movement with its seasoning of what is now sometimes called the higher pantheism. He recognised in full the value of the empirical and the deductive schools."

Mr. Bowen has shown that Carlyle's central truths regarding man's social and industrial evolution, the unity of humanity and God and the revelation of God in humanity, were expounded by Froebel; and that quotations might be made from Carlyle's works which even close students of Froebel might believe to have been written by him.

Mr. Hailman notes the similarity of the teachings of Herbert Spencer and Froebel in regard to the law of unification.

Dr. Harris says: "Froebel is the educational reformer who has done *more than all the rest* to make valid in education what the Germans call the developing method."

Mr. Bowen says: "Froebel is the true psychologist of childhood. Froebel alone translates psychological principles into psychological practice."

Dr. Harris says: "Froebel sees better than other educators the true means of educating the feelings, and especially the religious feelings"; and Dr. Hall, in speaking of Froebel's recognition of the fundamental nature of feeling as the foundation of intellect and will, says, "It is a great thought that now dominates psychology."

Dr. Harris, speaking of another phase of his educational philosophy—a most important one that Froebel really brought into human consciousness—says: "There is no philosophy for the young woman *to be compared with the philosophy that Froebel has put into his work on the mother's plays and games with her children.*"

In the recognition of God in Nature as the life in it and behind it and the evolutionary force in all things, organic and inorganic, Froebel has only one twin seer, Wordsworth, who gave to the world in exquisite song what Froebel a little earlier taught in prose.

Even the religious teachings that at first led the theologians to consider Froebel unorthodox are now recognised as the most vital truths revealed by Christ. Froebel was among the first to free religion from the formalism and the dogmatism that sapped its vitality.

The surest proof of true greatness in a philosopher is to find the leaders of the century succeeding his death climbing toward the light he saw and recognising his discoveries as everlasting and transforming truth.

CHAPTER II.

PESTALOZZI, HERBART, AND FROEBEL.

THE "new education" was undoubtedly revealed to the world chiefly by Pestalozzi, Herbart, and Froebel. If all other educational literature were destroyed, the principles of these three men would reveal all the vital forces that are moulding the educational systems and methods of to-day, both in aims and operations. The leaders of the epoch to which they belong seemed to be dominated by a similar spirit of investigation into the evolution of the human soul with the view of the general improvement of the race. A brief comparison of the systems and aims of these prophets of education will aid in understanding the relative value of Froebel's work.

With this end in view Froebel should be compared with Pestalozzi and Herbart separately.

Pestalozzi was instinctive and inspirational, Froebel was philosophical and investigative. Pestalozzi often applied correct principles without being conscious of their underlying philosophy or their adaptation to the nature of the child. Froebel studied the child for thirty years—in its mother's arms, on the playground, and as it exhibited its love of the beautiful and the wonderful in Nature. He also traced the development of the race, and compared it with the progressive unfolding of the powers of the child as it grew to manhood. Having exhaustively studied the child and history, he used the results of investigation and experience as a basis for his educational system. His foundation ideal was to bring the conscious educational processes of the schools into perfect harmony with the processes by which God develops the child so wonderfully, both in knowledge and in power, during the period of unconscious education before it goes to school.

Pestalozzi aimed to give definite ideas by the use of real things as a foundation for intellectual strength. Froebel provided the means of training the emotions as well as the sensations, and of guiding them in the formation of character by right self-activity.

Pestalozzi's pupils observed and *imitated* either with voice or hand; Froebel's children observed and *invented.*

Pestalozzi's pupils were reproductive; Froebel's were creative.

Pestalozzi's pupils were trained in expression; Froebel's in self-expression.

Pestalozzi was satisfied with productive activity; Froebel required productive self-activity. Carlyle caught Froebel's creative idea, when he said to each individual: "Be no longer a chaos, but a world or at least a worldkin. Produce! Produce! Were it but the pitifullest infinitesimal fraction of a product, produce it in God's name!"

Both these great teachers knew that the religious nature of man is the highest; but Froebel realized with much greater clearness than Pestalozzi the fact that spiritual growth must come from within, and that the spiritual nature of the child finds its satisfaction and growth in the symbolism of the real things around it. In his Mother Play he has given a definite and consecutive system, which is marvellous in its comprehensiveness and beauty, for defining the child's pure emotions, for enlarging its spiritual view, and for incidentally awakening its conceptions of its relationships and duties toward Nature, home, society, and God.

Pestalozzi was an intuitional philanthropist, who used education to make men wiser and happier. Froebel was an educational philosopher, who aimed through education to make men grow forever "consciously toward God."

Pestalozzi's ideal was, I must do good to the child. Froebel's ideal was, I must increase good through the child.

Herbart and Froebel were both more scientific than Pestalozzi in their methods of dealing with the subject of education. They worked out their systems logically and constructively; he was emotional and instinctive.

In their study of the child as the basis of a sound pedagogical system, Herbart and Froebel were in harmony in accepting the parallelism between the progress of the race and the development of the child. This idea was not original with either of them. Many of the ablest philosophers and theologians have held this view, and Rousseau and Pestalozzi had brought it within the range of educational discussion before the time of Herbart and Froebel. Froebel made more use than Herbart of this idea of similarity between the culture epochs in the growth of the individual and the race. It aided Herbart to decide what instruction is best suited to the child, the youth, the man, at different stages of his development; to Froebel it helped to reveal not only suitable material for instruction, but proper processes or occupations by which the child, the youth, and the man should define and increase knowledge and power and transform them into character.

Both Herbart and Froebel studied the child in order to lay down a system of education that would help to ennoble man and enable him to work out his highest destiny. They were fully in accord in regard to the true aim of education. Both made the development of moral character the great purpose of all education, and their study of the child was made to find the surest way to reach this desired end. There was a radical difference, however, in their attitude toward the child. Herbart studied the child to find the best that could be done for it; Froebel studied it to learn how it could be aided in working out its own best development. Herbart magnified the work of the teacher; Froebel magnified the work of the child. Herbart made instruction, and Froebel made self-activity, the source and cause of growth in knowledge and character.

The difference of view point leads to the chief distinction between the work of these two great educationists. Herbart discusses the work of the teacher, and shows what should be taught to the child, when it should be taught, and why it should be taught, with occasional suggestions as to how it should be taught. Froebel, on the other hand, considers chiefly the work of the child, and endeavours to lay down a complete system of education by which the child's entire nature may be called into vigorous exercise. Froebel keeps constantly in mind the work of the teacher, and he has clearly defined ideas regarding the order in which knowledge should be presented to the unfolding mind; but the basis of his pedagogical system is growth through self-activity of the child. He discusses the same problems as Herbart, but he reveals the child's part in the work of education, and tries to show the teacher how to guide the child in doing its own work without interfering with its spontaneity. Herbart improved the work of his predecessors, Froebel revolutionized it.

Herbart summarizes his entire pedagogical system in two brief sentences: "Instruction will form the circle of thought, and education the character. The last is nothing without the first. Herein is contained the whole sum of my pedagogy."

Having laid this foundation, he is naturally led to rely on the doctrine of interest as the central element in his pedagogical system. Interest, desire, action, will, is the order of the sequence of human development in his psychology. The doctrine of interest has been expounded by Herbart in a way that leaves little room for enrichment by his successors. With him interest is no passing fancy, no temporary attraction to things or subjects. It covers the whole ground of knowledge and of sympathy: "knowledge of the manifold, of its law, and of its æsthetic relations; sympathy with humanity, with society, and the relation of both to the highest Being." He describes interest as "the joy of life and the elevation of soul which knows how to part from life." He makes it, in the language of one of his greatest interpreters, Ufer, "the root of volition." He has been severely criticised for making action lead to will, instead of accepting the commonly received idea that will leads to action, but those who dissent most strongly from his views regarding the relationship of will and action may learn quite as much from his pedagogical use of interest as those who are his most ardent admirers. Opponents as well as disciples may have their ideas enlarged and defined by Herbart's discussion of interest, many-sidedness of interest, proportionate many-sidedness, empirical interest, speculative interest, æsthetic interest, sympathetic interest, social interest, religious interest, absorption, and reflection.

Herbart's system made instruction the basis of virtue. Ufer crystallizes Herbart's teaching on this point in the sentence: "When instruction has generated knowledge that incites to volition and that is controlled by ethical ideas its task is done."

It is easy to see how essential it was for Herbart to insist on apperception and correlation or co-ordination of studies. Apperception to Herbart meant more than the accumulation of knowledge, or even of new knowledge allied to what was already in the mind. It meant mind awakening, mind activity, mind defining, and mind enlargement, not by accretion but by assimilation of the new knowledge with the corresponding mind contents to form a greater mind content which should be a unity and not an aggregation of related ideas.

The law of unity led Froebel to insist even more strongly than Herbart on the perfect articulation and harmonious correlation of studies. He criticised severely the lack of unity in the studies of the school he attended when a boy, and endeavoured to remedy this defect in a school in which he taught while a student in Berlin. In all his after work he made unity an essential. He made this law of unity the basis of his kindergarten system. Every detail of his system in the gifts, occupations, games, songs, and stories is related to this central thought. To those who see behind the material and the occupations, the kindergarten is the objective embodiment of true concentration, and Froebel strongly urged that this same principle of correlation should dominate the arrangement of school programmes and the methods of teaching in the schools.

Froebel's view of the human soul was directly opposite to that held by Herbart. Froebel believed that the child has within him a self-active soul—an element of divinity, the selfhood or individuality of the child—and that this develops by being put forth in gaining a knowledge of its environment and in performing the duties pertaining to its social relationships. These opinions led him to discover his law of spontaneity or self-activity, which he made the underlying principle of all his developing and teaching processes in the kindergarten and in the school.

He did not mean by this law of spontaneity that the child has to acquire all knowledge by itself without the aid of the teacher. He gave instruction its true value. He did mean, however, that no instruction really becomes a content of the child's mind in the highest sense until the child has made a creative use of it in some way. Froebel's lessons always have two parts, the instructive and the creative. The teacher gives new instruction, and immediately the child makes an original use or application or modification of it. In this way, by his law of self-activity, Froebel secures to the fullest possible extent active, co-operative interest, and the most productive apperception. The child must be more interested and more definitely attentive when using knowledge than it can possibly be in receiving knowledge. Executive attention must be more developing than receptive attention, even if the pupil acts in carrying out the plans of the teacher; it becomes still more productive when the pupil executes his own plan or carries out his own design.

In discipline and training Herbart was much more coercive than Froebel, although less so than most of his predecessors and some of his successors. He made a much larger use of compulsion, both in forcing attention to study and in controlling the conduct, than Froebel. Froebel recognised the selfhood of the child as the true source of interest and the surest controlling force. He would not check effort, because he desired above all else positivity of character. He would not stop the current of real individual energy, he would change its direction when it was wrong by changing the pupil's centre of interest. His constant purpose was to secure reform and progress through the child so that it might become self-directing and self-progressive. Herbart recognised with great clearness the necessity for control; Froebel saw the harmony between spontaneity and control, "the perfect law of liberty." Yet Herbart acknowledged the individuality of the child. He wrote many wise things about it. He says, for instance, "The teacher ought to make it a point of honour to leave the individuality as untouched as possible." He criticises severely those teachers who "dominate the feelings of the pupil, and, holding him by this bond, unceasingly disturb the youthful character to such an extent that it can never know itself." But even his disciples acknowledge the fact that there is at least an apparent incongruity between his conception of the mind of the child as built up "entirely of presentations" and a true recognition of individuality. Herbart himself saw this. It is clearly impossible to give individuality its full recognition, when the conception of the soul is reduced to the smallest possible degree. The more the soul idea is limited, the less important does individuality become and the more potent does the teacher become as a decider of destiny. Froebel's conception of the soul as an element of divinity of the child gave him a reverence for individuality so profound that he demanded of the mother and teacher two things for the child—freedom and opportunity for creative activity in applying and extending the knowledge gained by experience and instruction.

The characteristics of the systems of Herbart and Froebel may be summarized as follows:

Both Herbart and Froebel made high moral character the great purpose of education. Herbart limited the original capacity of the human soul to one power, "that of entering into relations of the external world," or, as De Garmo defines Herbart's idea, "He assigned to the soul merely the capacity of self-preservation." Froebel regarded the soul as a germ of divinity, that must inevitably develop in power, and that should develop by its own creative self-activity. Herbart studied the child to mould it; Froebel studied it to guide it in its growth. Herbart studied the child as a philosopher; Froebel studied it as a sympathetic philosopher. Herbart's recognition of individuality was limited by his conception of the inherent powers of the soul; Froebel's idea of the child soul necessarily led him to reverence individuality as the central element in human development and as the thing that made the increase of human power desirable. Herbart saw the need of control much more clearly than the need of freedom; Froebel saw the harmony between freedom and control. Herbart made instruction the basis of virtue; Froebel made morality depend on true living in the home and in the school, on the awakening of the ideal as a counterpoise to the sensual, and on the recognition of and reverence for the life principle in and behind Nature. Herbart made will result from action; Froebel made action result from will. Self-activity developed the will according to Froebel, but the will increased in power as the result of its exercise in causing creative self-activity.

Herbart's contributions to pedagogy are a matchless discussion of interest, a thorough exposition of apperception, and a philosophic foundation for co-ordination of studies so that they may produce the most definite and most beneficial results on character. Froebel revealed the law of creative self-activity as the source of growth, including in it the most intense and most certain interest and the most perfect apperception, and the law of universal unity, in which unity of studies (correlation or concentration) was definitely recognised, although it is not the most important part of Froebel's comprehensive idea of unity.

Herbart aimed to produce in his pupils the spirit and the power of co-operative and productive activity. In this ideal he was the peer of all other educators except Froebel, and the superior of most of them. Froebel's ideal was co-operative, productive, and *creative* self-activity.

Perhaps Froebel's most distinctive characteristics were his comprehensive recognition of the deepest philosophy of the sages in regard to complete human development and his extraordinary power of translating this philosophy into a practical system of pedagogy, adapted alike to the symbolic period of unconscious childhood and the conscious growth of maturer years. Clear insight is good, high achievement is far better.

CHAPTER III.

FROEBEL'S FUNDAMENTAL LAW; UNITY OR INNER CONNECTION.

FROEBEL had one universal law to which he related all educational processes, by which he tested all educational methods, and on which he founded all educational principles. He believed absolutely that God created all things in a universal, interdependent, interinfluencing, ever-progressive harmony, a living unity of which God himself was and is and shall forever remain the centre and the spiritual essence, the divine source of life and light. No other words meant so much to him as *inner connection.* The fulness of their meaning it was his highest aim to reveal to his fellow-men, because to him they contained not only the true basis of systems and methods in education, but the philosophical principle on which the social organization should rest, and in conformity with which the progress of civilization must be made.

As he understood it, unity is the centre of all philosophy and the co-ordinating element in all life processes in the work of Nature and of man. To gain an insight into this vital and universal law Froebel's own words should be carefully studied. These words may at first seem mystical, but when reread and applied to the unities already fixed in the mind by experience they will gradually be understood, and will prove to be the language of a prophet soul who saw beyond his time. The mysticism will disappear with the defining and enlargement of our own apperceptive centres of relatedness.

The opening paragraph of his Education of Man reads as follows: "In all things there lives and reigns an eternal law. To him whose mind, through disposition and faith, is filled, penetrated, and quickened with the necessity that this can not possibly be otherwise, as well as to him whose clear, calm mental vision beholds the inner in the outer and through the outer and sees the outer proceeding with logical necessity from the essence of the inner, this law has been and is enounced with equal clearness and distinctness in Nature (the external), in the spirit (the internal), and in life, which unites the two. This all-controlling law is necessarily based on an all-pervading energetic, living, self-conscious, and hence eternal unity. . . . This unity is God."

In other places he writes: "Education consists in leading man, as a thinking, intelligent being, growing into self-consciousness, to a pure and unsullied, conscious and free representation of the inner law of divine unity, and in teaching him ways and means thereto."

"I would educate human beings who with their feet stand rooted in God's earth, in Nature, whose heads reach even into heaven and there behold truth, in whose hearts are united both earth and heaven, the varied life of earth and Nature, and the glory and peace of heaven, God's earth and God's heaven."

"The desire for unity is the basis of all genuinely human development and cultivation."

"The school endeavours to render the scholar fully conscious of the nature and inner life of things and of himself, to teach him to know the inner relations of things to one another, to the scholar, and to the living source and conscious unity of all things—to God."

"Never forget that the essential business of the school is not so much to teach and to communicate a variety and a multiplicity of things as it is to give prominence to the ever-living unity that is in all things."

"Every individual being, if it would attain its destiny, in necessary and indispensable obedience to its nature, must manifest and reveal itself in this triune way, in and as unity, in and as individuality, in and as manifoldness in ever-continuing diversity."

"Nature must be shown to the pupil as an organized and organic whole in all directions."

"Are not man and Nature the creatures of the one God? Must we not on this account necessarily find unity and harmony and obedience to the same law in the spirit of Nature and in the spirit of man, in external forms and forces, and in internal formation and thought?"

"Mathematics is the expression of the inner cause and of the outer limitations of space. As it originates in unity, it is in itself a unity; and, as space implies diversity in direction, shape, and extension, it follows that number, form, and magnitude mutually imply one another, and are an inseparable three in unity."

"The keystone of the kindergarten activity is the transformation of material, and therefore the perception of the *mutual connectedness* of the various solid forms, their derivation from one another, and the connection of all with the primary unity of space."

"Living soul unity sees life as an unbroken whole in all its operations and phenomena."

"The search for details is the more interesting the more fully a relatively greater unit has been previously grasped, though this need by no means be the greatest possible whole."

"The firmament, if anything, leads us to recognise the connection of all that is, and leads us up to unity—God. No one of the heavenly bodies is isolated, every planet has its centre in the sun of its system. All the solar systems are in relation and continual interaction with each other. That is the condition of all life. Everywhere mutual relation of parts. As above, in great things, an unbroken connection and harmony rule, so also here below, even in the smallest thing, everywhere is the same order and harmony, because the same law rules everywhere, the one law of God, which expresses itself in thousandfold many-sidedness, *but in the last analysis is one*, for God himself is the law. . . . Everywhere in God's creation, in the infinite manifoldness of phenomena, we always come upon unity, and must infer it where we do not perceive it."

"To reach the unconscious harmony of Nature, with consciousness in the human sphere, is the goal which God has set for man."

"Every productive work, every work consciously willed, is conditioned upon the union of parts according to an idea, and that is nothing else than organizaing."

"The time has come when man must recognise his relations to Nature, to the material world, and at the same time to the Spirit of God which rules in them."

Dr. Harris, in the introduction to The Education of Man, says: "There must be an inner connection between the pupil's mind and the objects which he studies, and this shall determine what to study. There must be an inner connection in those objects among themselves which determines their succession and the order in which they are to be taken up in the course of instruction. Finally, there is an inner connection within the soul that unites the faculties of feeling, perception, phantasy, thought, and volition, and determines the law of their unfolding."

Mr. Bowen faithfully interprets Froebel's central purpose when he says: "He [Froebel] pleads for the unification of *thought* and the unification of *life* by means of the unification of the materials of thought, and the unification of the preparation for life."

Mr. Hailman summarizes Froebel's fundamental law thus: "In his educational work this principle of life—unity—was ever uppermost in Froebel's mind. With reference to the individual human being, this *unification of life* means to Froebel harmony in feeling, thinking, willing, and doing; with reference to humanity, it means subordination of self to the common welfare and to the progressive development of mankind; with reference to Nature, it means a thoughtful subordination to her laws of development; with reference to God, it means perfect faith as Froebel finds it realized in Christianity."

Miss Blow, in her work on Symbolic Education, says: "The application of the idea of development to education has been in large measure the work of Pestalozzi and Froebel. To the former we owe the ideal of education as the harmonious development of inherent powers; to the latter must be accorded the honour of having first clearly perceived *the manifold implications of this ideal.* The mind of Pestalozzi was a battle ground between the idea of development and the atomism he had inherited from Rousseau. Over the mind of Froebel *the new ideal held the sole and supreme sway,* and so clear to him was its paramount significance that he could boldly affirm he would rather win from a tiny sand grain the history of its development than learn from God himself the structure of the universe."

These are the opinions of Froebel's best English-speaking interpreters, and they give to him the high honour of revealing to the world in applied form the law of unity, interrelationship, inner connection, "unification of life," development, or evolution. This law as Froebel understood it is too comprehensive in its varied meanings and applications to be fitly named by one word or phrase, or even by a series of words and phrases. It is great enough to form a life study, and it is so truly the basis of the evolutionary unification of life that as each year of progressive study widens the range of intellectual vision it reveals itself in extended applications and more harmonious co-ordinations. In a single chapter it is possible to give only a brief exposition of those applications of the law that should lead teachers to a broader conception of the meaning of education and aid them in gaining a fuller comprehension of the principles that underlie the art of teaching.

Speaking generally, the law is based on the idea that there is a central, co-ordinating, life-producing, life-giving, creative power, which is not only the source of all life and power, but is itself the life and power and evolutionary element in all creation; and that as this central power is itself perfect, the universal tendency of all life is a progressive development toward the divine unity in the evolution of ultimate perfection. "It is the destiny and life work of all things to unfold their essence, hence their divine being."

Confining the application of the law of unity to individual man, and especially to his educational growth, Froebel says: "It is the special destiny and life work of man, as an intelligent and rational being, to become fully, vividly, and clearly conscious of his essence, of the divine effluence in him, and therefore of God; to become fully, vividly, and clearly conscious of his destiny and life work; and to accomplish this, to render it (his essence) active, to reveal it in his own life with self-determination and freedom." As every human being has within himself the divine, the great work of education is to keep this divine essence in conscious unity with the divinity, so that by free self-activity it may achieve self-revelation, and, having found its own individuality, may define it in creative work for the race, of which greater organic unity it constitutes a complete, a free, but a responsible part.

Froebel taught that, if man at every stage of his evolution receives the training and culture suitable for his development at that time and adapted to the interested employment of his own powers, his spiritual relationship to the universal unity of humanity and God will unfold itself naturally through the symbolism of the material unities that are gradually revealed to him. He saw very clearly the inner connection or life unity existing between childhood, boyhood, youth, and manhood, and, applying the universal law, that a perfect organism can only be produced by the co-ordination of individually perfect parts or elements, he decided that the degree of perfection attained by each succeeding stage in the evolution of manhood must depend on the completeness of the appropriate development of the preceding stage or stages. The only possible preparation for a perfect development of boyhood is the complete unfolding of the powers of childhood; the characteristic evolution of childhood and boyhood prepares the way for the thorough training of youth; and the possibility of realizing a true manhood depends on the fulness of the fitting preparation made during the three previous stages of development.

If during the period of childhood the child is denied any of the conditions or opportunities of perfect child unfolding, or if it is forced or permitted to do or learn any of the work properly belonging to a later stage, the evil done can not be undone in the future by any process of training, however wise it may be. The dwarfing of omission and the blighting of wrong commission are permanent. "The child, the boy, man, indeed, should know no other endeavour but to be at every stage of development wholly what this stage calls for."

This is the doctrine of Froebel. In its extension this doctrine has led to the important modern investigations regarding nascent periods or life epochs of special aptitude for the study of certain subjects.

The violation of this doctrine has led to many of the worst errors in connection with education. The giving of abstract lessons in arithmetic and the attempts to develop mechanical expertness in arithmetical operations before space relationships have been incidentally defined in children's minds by using material things—not for the direct purpose of teaching arithmetic at all, but in carrying out some plan of building or other interesting process of self-activity—have made arithmetical dwarfs out of thousands who should have been mathematical giants. Arithmetical relationships and processes unfold themselves as naturally as the power of speech, in the minds of children who are led by their home and school occupations to form concepts of real mathematical relationships before they are asked to deal with mere mathematical symbols.

Froebel was far in advance even of those who imagine that they are fulfilling the requirements of pedagogical laws by using objects to represent number, in order to teach numerical conceptions, combinations, and operations. The lesson to be learned is not the direct object in Froebel's introductory work. The things used by the child are always more than mere number emblems. To use objects only as counters or as separate units follows the law of atomism or unrelated individualism, but it directly violates Froebel's law of unity. Even when the separate units are collected to represent number or combinations of numbers they are not associated in harmony with any law of "inner connection." They form an aggregation, not a true interrelated unity. There is no bond of life, no underlying interpenetrating idea around which they are organized. Objective representation of number is undoubtedly better than its abstract presentation to the child mind, but Froebel gave the child organized material which it can use in representing or expressing its own design or thought, and by the use of which it incidentally forms exact mathematical conceptions, which are as clear to its mind as any other conceptions received through its interesting plays or occupations. In this way arithmetic becomes attractive at the proper time, and the solution of problems is a source of stimulating interest.

The teaching of the formal rules of grammar too early often destroys the joy and the development that should come to the child through self-expression by language; and the attempt to teach botany, entomology, or zoölogy to young children robs them of the many advantages they should derive from their natural love of flowers, insects, and animals. It is a gross error to try to interest children in the scientific analysis and classification of flowers, insects, and animals, while they should simply be gaining through love of these things a clear recognition of the spirit of life in and behind them, and a consciousness of the ascending evolution of life in them. Their loving interest in these playfellows will form a basis for thorough and practical study of botany, entomology, and zoölogy in due time. The love of life developed in the child forms the only true basis for the scientific study of life by the boy or the youth. If a young man or woman begins the study of botany without having had the love and nurture of flower life developed in childhood by living with the flowers and, if possible, by planting their seeds and caring for them, the study will be formal and uninteresting. It will be carried on without the apperceiving centre of knowledge and the interest stimulus of love.

Froebel's principle of stage evolution holds as truly in the department of moral training as in intellectual culture. No greater wrong can be inflicted upon a child than to try to make it exhibit the characteristics of the religious life of maturity, either in profession or practice. The only certain product of such training is a hypocrite—the meanest thing that false training can make out of a being formed in God's image. There are two ways by which it may be made impossible for a man ever to become as true a type of Christian character as under proper conditions he might have been. The one is by starving his sympathies, his poetic fancy, and his artistic instincts while a child and leaving him without heart consciousness of love, formed in the loving home, and head consciousness of life, gained from the life in and behind Nature. The other is by forcing on him the religious principles and dogmas of a matured theology, or requiring from him the Christian service of adults.

But, although Froebel urges so strongly the absolute necessity for adequate and appropriate development in each stage of growth from infancy to manhood, he protests very forcibly against making "sharp limits and definite subdivisions within the continuous series of the years of development." Man's complete life unity must have continuity as well as unity. Indeed continuity is an essential element in Froebel's conception of every progressive unity. "That which follows," he says, "is always conditioned upon that which goes before." The present, in time or action, is always the link between the past and the future. Continuity is an essential in every progressive process. Man's development is not to be regarded as a series of distinct steps, but as a closely interrelated series of evolutionary degrees proceeding from infancy, and each a necessary preparation for the perfection of the succeeding degree. Each intermediate degree depends on its predecessor and prepares for its successor, and thus realizes Froebel's ideal of unity as connectedness.

Froebel broadly outlines the process of development in man in the sentence, "To make the internal external, and the external internal, to find unity for both, this is the general external form in which man's destiny is expressed." To childhood and the home he assigns the work of making the internal external. This includes the kindergarten period, as he hoped to have the kindergarten spirit in the homes, and aimed to make the kindergartens themselves in reality co-operative homes for children—homes in which there should be the unity of social conditions among the children and the unity of culture, wisdom, and motherliness in the kindergartners. The second and third periods, boyhood and youth, during which the external is to be made internal and unity discovered and defined between the internal and the external, are to be spent in school (including college). The first period he calls the period of *life*, the second the period of *learning*, the third the period of *unification*. During the first period the child makes the acquaintance of Nature, defines its own powers, and strengthens its selfhood by putting its inner life out in its plays and by gaining constructive control over its material environment in its voluntary and directed occupations. During the second period it should receive a well-chosen and well-organized course of instruction; and during the third it should be led to see itself in its relationships to the material world, to society, and to God. The germ feelings and thought or apperceptive centres for the complete development of the third period should be evolved in the first period and the body of knowledge organized so as to aid in the culture of mind, and the formation of character should be communicated during the second period. Then, in the third period the unification of the internal with the external is consciously revealed, reason is developed, desire transformed into will, and "will into firmness of will," or stability of uptending character.

These three stages of growth thus outlined by Froebel in very general terms correspond closely, first, to the period spent at home before going to school, when spontaneity or free life activity predominates in the child's development; second, to school life, when the boy is instructed; and, third, to college life, during which the youth should be made conscious of his own individual relationships and responsibility, and trained to reason properly, that he may have a reliable inner guide to direct his life work.

Froebel would make as radical changes in the third stage in the evolution of perfect manhood as he did in the first. He would make a college much more than a higher school for giving instruction in special departments of learning. The college should train manhood. The chief aim of college training should be constructive character work, rather than the giving of extended intellectual culture alone. The best intellectual culture would be secured by giving character construction the first, and mind storing the second place. Young men should not be mere atoms in a great college aggregation, they should be responsible, self-directing individuals in a great unity whose "inner connection" should be the fuller comprehension of duty based on relationship to their fellow-men and God. The gradual revelation of universal interdependence in the consciousness is a mightier stimulus to self-activity or individual effort (the only true productive effort) for culture than the external incentives of competitive examination, class standing, or scholarships. These, according to Froebel's philosophy, are not only weak, as all purely external incentives are, but destructive of true character, as they develop the immoral competitive spirit instead of the spirit of community. Whatever weakens the bond of human unity is evil; whatever strengthens it is divine in quality and tendency. Froebel would therefore give to youth in the third stage of human evolution much more freedom of action than is now given in most colleges and universities, as the only basis for the natural development of social relationship and responsibility. He understood the harmony between the control of parent, kindergartner, teacher, or professor and the spontaneity of the child, boy, or youth so fully that he had a sacred reverence for individual freedom. This harmony between control and spontaneity was part of his law of unity, as was his recognition of the harmony between all apparent opposites He demanded such reverence for individual selfhood as would give more freedom to the pupil in every stage of his development, and in the third stage he would enlarge freedom into conscious liberty as the source of conscious responsibility. The old mandatory dominating spirit of college and university control must change. It may be changed safely, when the evolution of childhood and boyhood is in harmony with the true principles of child and boy development.

Speaking of his own training at Jena, during his third stage of development, he said: "My stay at Jena had taught me much; but by no means so much as it ought to have taught me, but yet *I had won for myself* a standpoint both subjective and objective. I could already perceive unity in diversity, the correlation of forces, the interconnection of all living things, life in matter, and the principles of physics and biology." Examination could test only the least important of these acquirements.

Writing of his own conscious mental development, he said: "The most pregnant thought which arose in me at this period (aged twenty-five) was this: All is unity, all rests in unity, all springs from unity, strives for and leads up to unity, and returns to unity at last. This striving in unity and after unity is the cause of the several aspects of human life." Three years later he wrote, "Mankind as a whole, as one great unity, has now become my quickening thought"; and again, two years afterward, he wrote of the lectures of Prof. Weiss, of Berlin, on natural history, "The lectures for which I had so longed really came up to the needs of my mind and soul and awakened in me, more fervent than ever, the certainty of the demonstrable inner connection of the whole cosmical development of the universe."

The conception of unity grew more clear to him, till it became the guiding element in his life work. He continued without ceasing to "systematize, symbolize, idealize, realize, and recognise identities and analogies among all facts and phenomena, all problems, expressions, and formulas which deeply interested him; and in this way life, with its varied phenomena and activities, became to him more and more free from contradictions, more harmonious, simple, and clear, and more recognisable as a part of the life universal."

Filled with this great ideal, the natural step next in order was to plan for making his conception of the great unity clear to his fellow-men. While walking on the banks of the Rhine, where the Main pours in its waters, and surrounded by "Nature at her loveliest and freshest," the thought came to him, "There must exist somewhere some beautifully simple and certain way of freeing human life from contradiction, some means of restoring to man *himself at peace internally*." To seek out this way became the vocation of his life.

Seeing the advantages of a living unity so clearly, it is not strange that he should regard unification of knowledge, and conscious interrelationship as the supreme work of the training of a young man or woman. For this fullest preparation for the conception of duty and the independent power to execute it, he planned the course of education in the three stages of human evolution. He wrought out in detail only the first, but the foundation law throughout he believed to be unity, and the fundamental process self-activity.

There is no doubt that the extensive attention now paid to the investigation of the theory of "culture epochs" will lead to a much fuller understanding of Froebel's law of evolution and a more definite classification of the stages or degrees or life epochs in human development; but whatever discoveries may be made in this department of pedagogy, Froebel must always be regarded as the first to make the theory of "culture epochs" a part of pedagogical practice. He regarded it as of such supreme importance that he wrote: "If the moment of the natural budding of the new subject of instruction has been missed, every later attempt arbitrarily to introduce the subject lacks interest. . . . The distinctive character of a natural and rational life-stirring and developing system of instruction lies in the finding and fixing of this point. For when it is truly found, the subject of instruction grows independently in accordance with its own living law, and truly teaches the teacher himself. Therefore, the whole attention of the teacher must be directed to these budding points of new branches of instruction." The most advanced modern investigation has not got beyond Froebel in the theory of nascent periods or culture epochs.

Froebel applied the law of unity to the development of man's physical, intellectual, and spiritual powers in harmony. This view of individual unity is now very generally accepted in theory, although still almost universally violated in practice. The usual practice is to make definite and systematic effort to develop the intellectual powers, or at least store the minds of pupils, but few schools make equally definite and systematic efforts to train their bodies and develop their spiritual powers. Froebel taught that bodily activity and the condition of the vital organs has a direct influence on the development of the brain and nervous system, and on the co-ordination of the brain, the nervous system, and the body itself. Modern neurology sustains his theory. He taught that the essential elements necessary to form a strong character are a vigorous active body; a well-developed, well-nourished, co-ordinated brain as the organ of a balanced mind; and a spiritual nature sympathetically responsive to truth, purity, and nobility in man, to beauty, life, and evolution in Nature and to the love and inspiration of God. He believed that these elements of true manhood should be trained as a unity; that God had created them in harmony; and that those who train one department only of man's nature at the expense of the other two are producing abnormal beings, out of harmony with God's plan. This is so absolutely true that the tendency of Nature is to refuse to reproduce such abnormal men and women. Herbert Spencer says: "A deficiency of reproductive power in women results from overtaxing their brains." Mr. Spencer shows narrowness in attributing loss of reproductive power as the result of overtaxing the brain to women only. Mr. Galton found a similar result among men of genius. It is quite as true in the case of men as of women. This result, however, does not necessarily follow from the complete development of the brain or its vigorous and sustained action, but from the culture and exercise of the brain *at the expense of the body.* Mr. Spencer evidently believes that the evil springs from anomalous development, because he holds that "physical labour makes women less fertile," although he thinks more evidence is needed to prove this conclusively. It is reasonable to conclude that the destructive or restrictive effects of physical overexertion on fertility, or on any other bodily function, are not so great or so immediately recognisable as the effects of overstimulation and overexertion of the brain. Bodily exertion develops the brain to a considerable extent, and so tends to preserve the necessary harmony of development, but overactivity of the brain prevents the proper development of the body and directly interferes with harmonious development or the perfect unity that Froebel desired to restore and perpetuate as a basis for complete happiness and the conscious evolution of the race toward the divine. The prolonged intensification of great intellectual effort and the neglect of physical training must lead to the weakening of the vital organism, the disorganization of the nervous system, the deterioration of physical energy, and therefore to a "deficiency of reproductive power." The law of unity is so absolute and inexorable that its violation is always followed by appropriate penalty.

The destruction of the natural harmony between the physical, intellectual, and spiritual powers by overstraining or overexerting any department of human power at the expense of the others is inevitably evil in its effects. There are men and women who have possessed, and do now possess, extraordinary intellectual power, and whose physical culture has been entirely neglected. Some notable instances have occurred in which the brain of a genius has been lodged in a body feeble from birth. These illustrations do not disprove the correctness of the law of unity of development. On the contrary, they confirm it in a most emphatic manner. In every such case the great intellectual work is performed by the aid of the energy stored up by generations of ancestors, and at the expense of the succeeding generation. The second, if not the first generation, in such cases is childless, or the number of children is small, and those who are born rarely possess much strength either of body or mind. Every teacher who stimulates the intellectual powers of her pupils without definitely and systematically training the physical powers and the spiritual powers at the same time is fighting against God.

The educational aims and methods of the past, by directing attention almost exclusively to the intellect and by training the sensor at the expense of the motor system, have done violence to the law of unity between the physical, intellectual, and spiritual powers. The evil effects would have been much more clearly seen but for the fact that the children have had opportunities for natural development outside of school. They are more easily discoverable in cities, where the pupils have fewer opportunities for free activity and for direct contact with the life and beauty of Nature than are enjoyed by children who are fortunate enough to live in the country.

Froebel understood the unity between feeling, knowing, and willing. In the evolution of the individual man he recognised not only the continuity between the stages of his development and the unity between his physical, intellectual, and spiritual powers, but, dealing with the intellectual powers only, he considered them to be a unity in their action, and by advocating this view he helped to do away with the old theory that the intellectual powers consisted of a number of independent faculties, each of which required a distinct time and special process for its development.

But one of his most important discoveries in regard to the unities of the individual man was that there should be harmony between man's receptive, reflective, and executive powers. He improved upon the motto of Comenius, "Children learn to do by doing." To Froebel growth was always greater than learning. He did not undervalue learning, but he valued it as an aid to growth, so as he interpreted the motto of Comenius it gained increased significance and became, "Children *grow* by doing." His process of self-activity is based on the principle that development comes not alone from doing, but from doing under the direct and original guidance of the mind of the doer. The act is the execution of the decision of the mind, based on the knowledge already stored in it. True self-activity does acquire knowledge more rapidly than any other process, but it does more than acquire knowledge, it apperceives it and organizes it with the kindred knowledge already in the mind. The only way that the knowledge in the mind can certainly be roused into aggressive expectancy for the reception of new knowledge is by self-activity, which requires the inceptive process of learning to take place in the mind. But Froebel accomplished more than learning by self-activity. He developed the selfhood and made it not only receptive and reflective, but executive. He taught that to destroy the unity that naturally exists between this trinity of power prevents the full development of each individual power, and weakens character by making it negative instead of positive. Receptivity and reflection are never so active or so definite in the mere acquisition of an idea as in the expression or representation or execution of the idea. The development of the first two steps in the sequence is of little use to the individual or to humanity unless the third is developed as well.

The tendency of little children, even after centuries of weakening of executive or motor force by the almost exclusive training of the sensory system, is to carry out their decisions at once. All day long with sand or sticks or stones or improvised spades or other tools, if they are free and have the good fortune to be allowed to "play in the dirt," they experiment with the properties of material things, and immediately execute their decisions and designs in building, tunnelling, and all kinds of engineering operations. Some anxious parents are discouraged because at this period their children change so quickly from one plan to another, showing an apparent lack of persistence in work. Persistence is not the quality the child is developing. Its attention flits from plan to plan, but it at least attempts to carry out every plan it forms. The same heap of sand may form the material for a score of plans in a day, but the child makes its own plans and carries them out in its own imperfect way. It is a pity that the unity between decision and action is ever broken. Froebel would strengthen the bond until it becomes conscious and till men cease to form decisions, merely to fail to execute them from lack of will and executive habit. To preserve and strengthen this unity by developing the missing link, executive habit, should be one of the primary aims of all teachers.

Froebel taught that unity was the only possible basis for the development of the race as well as of the individual. "Only humanity as a whole, as a unit, can fully attain the highest and ultimate purpose of human striving, the representation of pure humanity." He believed, with many educators and philosophers who had preceded him, that the race had culture epochs corresponding to those he defined in the evolution of the individual, and that the true culture of the race required similar continuity of development to that of the individual. But Froebel taught that the evolution of the race depended on a unity between the individual and the race much more intimate and more vital than the mere correspondence of their culture epochs. He believed that each individual should be the ideal of the organized race; or, in other words, that individual man can never be a perfect individual until he has in his mind a clear conception of the perfect type of the totality of the race in complete unity; and that race perfection will only be possible when the individuals composing it shall all be race-inclusive unit wholes. This original, doubly interrelated conception of race community, based on the interstimulating unity of the individuals composing it, and of the unity of the individual as representing in himself the fullest evolution of the race, is the highest ideal of interrelationship between man and mankind ever conceived. It is still so advanced a thought that the English language contains no word or phrase that adequately expresses Froebel's conception of the race-comprising man, the whole-including unit. How sublimely perfect is the ideal of community that conceives a unity of race-revealing men! How great a thought this is for an educational ideal!

Froebel fixed no limit of time for the realization of this ideal. He knew that individual and race evolution must be gradual, but he knew also that race deterioration would continue until the effort of the race was made toward a true ideal. His educational aim was to give each individual power to achieve the best culture of the race up to date, a matured consciousness of race relationship, and a joyous sense of the highest privilege of a human being—to aid humanity in its upward evolution. This ideal gives a new glory to individuality and adds dignity to manhood. Already there are evidences to show that it is beginning to revolutionize theological as well as educational ideals. In revealing the majesty of the child and the community of mankind—the perfect unity between individualism and socialism—Froebel is Christ's truest interpreter.

Froebel made the inner connection between Nature, man, and God the basis of the early study of Nature, and the foundation on which he rested the child's first development in the recognition of life and its evolution, which in later years was to form one of the main centres with which its religious conceptions were to be associated. He aimed "to build up a life which should be everywhere in touch with God, with physical nature, and with humanity at large." He strongly emphasized the principle that "if man is fully to attain his destiny, so far as earthly development will permit this, if he is to become truly an unbroken living unit, *he must feel and know himself to be one, not only with God and humanity, but also with Nature."* He saw in the unity and evolution of Nature the best types for the revelation of spiritual unity and human evolution to the child. Material environment is the best revealer of the spiritual to the child, as it was to the race in its earliest stage of development. Even to the adult whose spirit is responsive to Nature, whose imagination can co-ordinate the harmonies of the universe, Nature ever speaks clearly, and is the best visible type of the invisible.

Froebel was not a pantheist, but he saw God in all things. Through Nature he would lead the child to see unity, and ultimately God as the source and centre of all unity, including itself. By a loving study and nurture of the life in Nature and of its gradual evolution toward higher types by culture and by the interfructification of the finest related specimens to form a unity of the fittest, he gave the idea of life unity and progressive development toward more perfect form and higher function. By the development of plant life in continuously improving forms he foreshadowed the later conception of the evolution of human life, and finally completed the ever-widening, ever-ascending sequence of life in God himself.

He believed that if children are brought up amid the life of Nature, in due time they become conscious of a moral strengthening from the surrounding nature, as definitely as they become conscious of physical strengthening from the surrounding atmosphere.

Froebel regarded a tree as the "most expressive symbol of all organization, whether of natural or of intellectual life." He found in each tree harmony within itself, a characteristic similarity between bark and trunk, and branches and leaves; individuality in the distinctive form and foliage of each kind of tree; variety (an essential in perfect unity) in the different parts and distinctions between different kinds of trees; and unity in the correspondences between all trees and all parts of the same tree. His type of unity in the solid was the sphere, and in plane figures the circle.

In a conversation with Diesterweg he gave perhaps the fullest statement of the interrelationships existing between God, man, and Nature. "What other objects of our knowledge exist," he asks, "but *God, man, Nature?* What other task can our intellect have than to find the relation between these three sole existing objects? The first thing for the human mind is to draw the synthesis *God in Nature, Nature from God* (the history of creation); then follows the synthesis *the Divine Spirit in humanity, the human spirit from God,* or the Christian revelation through Jesus Christ (God-man). Now, there is yet to be drawn the synthesis between *humanity* and *Nature,* and thus to recognize the triunity which makes up the result of this *connection* or unifying of *opposites.*"

Thus he made human life the unifying element in the triunity, the link between the unconscious life of Nature and the "all-conscious mind"; between the material nature and the spiritual God; as man possesses both the bodily and the spiritual natures, becoming more like God as his spiritual nature dominates the material.

Another and a most important phase of Froebel's all-comprehending law of unity is the reconciliation of apparent contradictions, the harmonizing of opposites, or the connection of contrasts. It constitutes the philosophical basis of the law of development or unification. It is sometimes spoken of as the law of mediation. Froebel usually spoke of it simply as the "law of opposites," and his estimate of its importance may be found in the brief statement, "The first law of all phenomena is the law of opposites." He used the word phenomena in this sentence in its most inclusive sense, as applied to the material, the intellectual, and the spiritual world. "Everything and every being comes to be known only as it is connected with the opposite of its kind, and as its unity, its agreement with this opposite, its equation with reference to this is discovered; and the completeness of this knowledge depends upon the completeness of this connection with the respective opposite, and upon the complete discovery of the connecting thought or link." Large and small, high and low, up and down, above and below, behind and before, inside and outside, right and left, forward and backward, hard and soft, light and heavy, old and young, good and evil, love and hate, beauty and ugliness, strength and weakness, generosity and meanness, health and sickness, freedom and slavery, are illustrations of the truth of Froebel's theory. It is impossible to conceive freedom without a consciousness of what restriction means. The child learns what freedom and restriction mean by noting the difference in the lives of animals and birds, and too often by bitter experience. It notes the difference between the free bird or squirrel or fish and those confined in cage or aquarium. The harnessed horse at work guided by the bridle or reins and the colt that roams at will in the field, and many other external illustrations, gradually make it conscious of freedom and restriction, and the knowledge of the one depends on the clearness with which the other is comprehended. In its own experience it gradually comes to realize the distinction between confinement in the house, or at school, or at work, and the freedom of play. Some of its plays, such as "prisoner's base," evidently had their origin in the unfolding of the ideal of freedom, and are a part of Nature's plan for revealing the conception of liberty. Through life everything that makes lack of freedom a more definite conception makes the idea of freedom more clear and complete. The cells in the Tower of London and the triple walls of the innermost dungeon of the old Spanish fort at St. Augustine, with its cruel chains and midnight darkness into which no ray of sunlight ever came, have helped to define the thought of liberty in the minds of all who have ever been in them.

As the child develops, its idea of bodily freedom gradually evolves into a conception of mental and spiritual freedom.

Health is never understood until sickness reveals its true meaning. Carlyle did not know he had a stomach till he was nearly thirty years of age, and then his dreadful enemy, dyspepsia, kept him in constant remembrance of the fact. So throughout the range of our knowledge—of time, space, dimension, colour, etc.—the knowledge is made clear by clear conception of opposites.

But Froebel considered the conception of opposites to be but the first step in true knowledge. The connection of the opposites is the completion of knowledge. The life of the knowledge is in the unification of the opposites.

Miss Blow says with much force: "An isolated fact is a *dead* fact; a fact seen only in its relations is still a dying fact; grasped in its total process it is a living and life-giving fact." Organization, linking together "thought in process," sequence, was the great aim of Froebel's education. The Mother Play abounds in plays which are but types of others, that he hoped mothers or educators would devise for children, and in which the process of linking together, especially the linking of the child with the family, Nature, society, and God is revealed not by words, but by activity; the deed laying the foundation of the thought. This he believed to be the true basis not only for profitable thinking but for logical reasoning. From the result to the cause the child proceeds step by step, learning social relationships and interdependence and the inner connection of all things; and learning to think logically at the same time. Speaking of the pat-a-cake play (baker), for instance, he says: "Does any other connection rule in philosophical deduction than the one I call the child to perceive in this game? The logic is and remains a consecutive thinking and conclusion, whether applied to the things themselves or to the abstract conceptions of things."

The so-called object teaching of England and America was utterly at variance with Froebel's fundamental law because it taught isolated facts by material things. He demanded for the child not only knowledge, but knowledge in use as part of a unified process. He used things in his system not that they might be studied, but that they might become a means of expressing the child's conceptions, on the one hand, and, on the other, of defining them in such a way under wise guidance as to reveal universal inner connection. The "discovery of the connecting thought or link" as a fundamental principle in philosophy and as a means of awakening the mind and widening its range of conscious activity was Froebel's educational purpose.

Froebel's system, so far as he had completed it, was planned to give every child very early in life an insight into the law of the reconciliation of opposites. Beginning with the ball as his first gift, he worked outward from it in a logical sequence through all his gifts. His principle of mediation is exemplified in his second gift, in which the cylinder, possessing some of the properties of both the ball and the cube, forms the connecting link between them. It is admirably revealed to the child by its own activity in his drawing processes, his stick laying, his paper pasting, and tablet and ring work, in each of which the child is led to produce most beautiful symmetrical designs by conforming to the law which unifies by bringing opposites into harmony about a centre or a series of centres. His colour work made the law a part of the child's experience by leading it to mix colours to produce other colours, and thereby helping it to recognize the law of unity in colour.

The play of The Bridge is intended to symbolize the reconciliation of contrasts. This thought is kept in view in all the detailed work he planned. His aim was, without specially directing the attention of the child to the fact, to make him live in a well-knit world in which, whatever path he took, he would find closely related experiences; so that he would live in an atmosphere of continuity which would prepare his mind for the clearer realization of the philosophy of unity and the unity of philosophy in maturer years. "The triple unity of God is obvious in all his works to eyes that can see. Have we not always and everywhere a trinity *composed of contrasts and their intermedium?*"

Froebel's conception of unity led him to see the need of the correlation of the subjects to be taught in school. This application of his fundamental law will be considered in a chapter specially devoted to itself.

By whatever name the law of unity may be described—development, evolution, continuity, connectedness, interrelationship, interdependence, interstimulation, or life unity—it is a vital law of psychology, of pedagogy, of philosophy, of life. Every phase of it is important. All its aspects are really one, in unity with each other, but applications of the same great principle. It applies to individual man in the continuity of the stages of his growth, in the relationships of his varied powers, and in the activity of his intellectual faculties; it applies to the interdependence of individual man in families, social groups, nations, and of all these in the community of the race, and the supreme unity of all in God. It is what he longed to find—"a certain way of freeing human life from contradiction and of restoring man to himself, at peace internally." It aims to make perfectly free, independent, self-directing, unity-recognizing individuals as the only way of securing a perfect humanity, an organized unity, perfect because each is a unity having within himself the best elements of racial development, and yet each possessing a distinct individuality of his own. The individual is never lost in Froebel's unity. The more strikingly diverse the individual elements are the more complete the unity. Contrasts and diversities are but complements to each other. Sameness is not unity.

He made unity the groundwork of all educational work, and his thought is beginning to guide the best educational investigation. He summarizes the educational aspects of the law in a pregnant sentence: "The knowledge of that eternal law, the insight into its origin, into its essence, into the totality, the connection and intensity of its effects, the knowledge of life in its totality, *constitute science, the science of life;* and, referred by the self-conscious, thinking, intelligent being to *representation* and *practice through and in himself,* this becomes the *science of education.*"

As has been beautifully pointed out by the Baroness von Bülow, Froebel by his law of unity aimed to accomplish more than is usually comprehended in the word education, although not more than Froebel himself meant by education. "All the domains of human life are necessarily penetrated with one spirit; and since they are linked together as independent organs, they must form conscious parts of the whole, which is human society." "To that end, at some future time, science and art, as well as all the active principles of human life, justice and religion (or state and Church), must be penetrated with the same spirit of truth and with a consciousness *of the one aim of serving humanity,* perfected according to the thought of God—that is, 'the kingdom of God upon eath.' This aim, mutual love, penetrating all individuals, must unite them into a living, self-conscious whole, which then represents a spiritualized or glorified humanity."

Such, indeed, was Froebel's aim, and to mothers and

teachers he looked for help in the gradual evolution of the race to the complete fulfilment of its high destiny. It is no vain theory. It is more than a pleasing but illusory vision of a transcendentalist. It may become a reality. There is in each child an element of the divine which renders it possible for it to attain a marvellous development in even a single generation. What limit dare man lay to the cumulated development of a race composed of such evolutionary individuals when the child and the myriad and multiplex agencies that mould it are studied so carefully that it may be truly guided in its upward growth by wise and noble teachers?

There are many indications to show that Froebel's idea of unity, Christ's idea of unity, is really becoming a dominant thought in human progress. Social, educational, and religious organization and co-ordination have been the greatest movements of the second generation since Froebel's death. Not only are these different elements uniting in leagues of various developing kinds within themselves, but a much higher kind of unification has begun by the co-ordinating of all the forces of human progress. Froebel's work will always plead for this co-ordination of effort around "the little child." The mothers' classes now being organized in all civilized countries by kindergartners are revivals of the conferences begun by Christ, when he "set a little child" in the centre of his group of students nineteen hundred years ago.

The rapid development of socialism and trades unions proves that the human mind is being penetrated with the thought of rising together. "In union is strength," is a part of the truth that Froebel taught.

Even the spread of individualism as opposed to socialism is a hopeful evidence of a movement toward ultimate right. It is the outcome of the realization by humanity of the dignity and the sacredness of its individuality. This must precede the final triumph of the race. Perfect individualism is the only basis for perfect socialism. Race-including men will unite to form a man-respecting race.

Froebel's law of unity is of practical value to teachers in many ways. It teaches the hopeful law of development, and therefore gives teachers a higher ideal and a more encouraging outlook. They are no longer instructors merely, they are character builders, who should be mighty agents in accomplishing the final unity of humanity, and of humanity with God. They no longer value knowledge more than the child who is to receive it.

It reveals the great importance of the study of childhood, boyhood, and youth, in order to learn definitely the nature of the culture epochs and nascent periods of each, and the best means of revealing knowledge, life unity, and duty at each stage of development. It specially shows the need of the preparatory symbolic education of the first period of child evolution.

It teaches that isolated knowledge is unproductive, and that it will not remain in the mind, even when relationship is shown by explanations or illustrations by the teacher. The living process of relationship must be thought out, and, if possible, wrought out by the pupil himself, in order to make the knowledge a positive element in character. This was Froebel's idea of apperception—active, positive apperception. It was also the basis of his law of correlation. Not only are "isolated facts dead facts," separated subjects have only a partial vitalizing power. Isolation always leads to death.

It teaches that it is wrong to give formal knowledge before laying a foundation for it by establishing apperceptive centres for it by experience. All teachers admit that the work of the teacher in educating a child must be based on the content of its mind. It is admitted also that the experiences of some children are wider and more productive of rich content than the experiences of others. Froebel would not leave any child's experiences to chance. He planned a comprehensive system of experiences to develop not only apperceptive centres of knowledge, to which other knowledge could be joined in vital unity, but also apperceptive insights of relationship and apperceptive motives of interest. Formal mathematics should not reveal space relations, but result from them. Science study should be based on a reverent love for the life of Nature. The science of language can not be profitably taught until conscious expression has become a joyous experience. Formal morality will deaden moral feeling, unless the concepts of life and love have been developed by the life of Nature and the love of home. Teachers should learn from the law of unity to value physical and spiritual development more highly, so highly that they will make as systematic efforts for their development as are now made to give intellectual culture. Until they do so the law of unity will be violated.

They should also learn the importance of training executive power as the only certain source of thorough training for the receptive and reflective powers, and the only means by which these powers can be made of service to the individual or to humanity.

The law of reconciliation of contrasts or opposites should enable teachers to understand the harmony between control and spontaneity. They should make this the foundation law of discipline. It is the "perfect law of liberty." Perfect spontaneity and complete submission to law are fond lovers. Every teacher should perform the ceremony of uniting these lovers in the life of the child. No teacher is fully qualified until prepared for this high service.

> Silently cherish your baby's dim thought
> That life in itself is as unity wrought.
> Make paths through which he may feel and may think
> That of this great whole he, too, is a link.
>
> *Froebel.*

CHAPTER IV.

FROEBEL'S FUNDAMENTAL PROCESS: SELF-ACTIVITY.

"Man is a creative being."—*Froebel.*

"Knowledge is food, but creation is life."—*Miss Blow.*

"We must launch the child from its birth into the free and all-sided use of its powers."—*Froebel.*

WHEN Froebel's law of creative self-activity is understood so thoroughly as to become a fundamental element in the practical work of teachers, it will be recognised as the most important law of method ever discovered. It is the universal test for good teaching and the unfailing revealer of bad methods. "Self-activity" and "spontaneity" become dead words unless the principles they represent are practised. All truth dies in the mind unless it is lived out in practice. No truth is clear to any individual until he has applied it. There are thousands of teachers who can define "self-activity" who never give their pupils an opportunity to be self-active.

One of the most important lessons for teachers is the distinction between activity and self-activity, between expression and self-expression, as revealed by Froebel. Froebel's law of self-activity meant much more than the law of Comenius as commonly understood, that "children learn to do by doing," or the common maxim, "Practice makes perfect." He distinguished very clearly between the activity of the child in response to the suggestion or instruction of its parents or teachers and activity in carrying out its own impulses or decisions. This distinction is the basis of the most comprehensive law of method in child development.

Froebel knew that the activity of the child itself, even when directed by the teacher, is better, infinitely better, than receptive passivity; but he believed that selfhood or individuality, like all other powers, must be developed by activity or "exercise of function," and he therefore gave to selfhood its rightful place as the guide of the child's powers when they are being exercised in learning. Other educators had developed certain of the child's powers by practice; he did this, but much more, by his law of self-activity. At the same time that he trained the individual powers of a child he developed its individuality. Individuality and the individual powers should be clearly distinguished. Individuality is the originating and controlling element that starts the individual powers to act, and guides them while at work. The power to work and the wisdom that enables us to work effectively are not enough to insure productive activity in character. The motive power of character is even more important than the operative power, and should be trained even more definitely. As motive power is higher than operative power, it is more susceptible to training.

Mr. Hailman, one of the most sympathetic of Froebel's interpreters, distinguishes Froebel's self-activity from the restricted ideal of other educators: "Self-activity, in Froebel's sense of the word, implies not merely that the learner shall do all himself, not merely that he will be benefited only by what he does; it implies that at all times his whole self shall be active, that the activity should enlist his entire self in all the phases of being. The law of self-activity demands not activity alone, but all-sided activity of the whole being, the whole self. Froebel's self-activity applies to the whole being; it would have all that is in the child self-actively growing, simultaneously and continuously."

Froebel's law of unity led him to believe that if the motive power and the operative power are not trained at the same time, neither can attain its best development. He did not think it wise to train the various operative powers separately, and then trust to chance for the development of the originating and directing powers to guide them. He taught that the originating and controlling powers must be developed by free exercise just as all other powers have to be developed, and that the operative powers act with greater vigour in response to internal than to external stimulation. In this way he saw that true self-activity, activity that originates in the mind of the individual who acts, is the most productive kind of activity in the development of operative power, controlling power, and originating power.

Several educators have seen the advantages of activity for the training of operative power; a few have noted its influence indirectly on the will or controlling power. Froebel alone saw that education is defective at its most vital point if the originating element of character is left untrained.

The development of educational aims has been a progressive series of advancing steps, first through the partial culture of the child's self, and later by a partial training by activity. Froebel aimed to give a complete training to self and the activity of self by the law of self-activity.

The child's powers may be classified as receptive, reflective, and executive. The receptive powers accumulate knowledge, the reflective powers classify knowledge and prepare it for use, the executive powers apply or use the knowledge gathered by the receptive powers and classified by the reflective powers. Executive power means more than administrative ability. It means power to execute well what we know, to do what we plan, to be in progressive action all we are in matured thought and defined feeling. It means man's power to control circumstances and mould them in harmony with great original purposes. It enables him to represent his best conceptions in productive activity. It is the power that impels a man to "do noble things, not dream them all day long." It decides his influence on his fellow-men as a co-operative agent working in harmony with God.

The history of educational progress may be divided into three periods based on the attention paid to the three classes of the child's powers. At first only the receptive powers were trained, then the reflective, and, finally, the executive powers or the activities. In the evolution toward complete self-activity there has been in each of the periods named a passive and an active stage. Whether educators aimed to develop the receptive, the reflective, or the executive powers, they began in each case by keeping the pupil in a passive or dependent position. This makes six distinct steps in the evolution of educational ideals.

In passive receptivity the pupil received knowledge from the teacher. Good teaching comprised good telling and good listening. The aim was the communication of knowledge. The ideal teacher was the one who could give most information in the shortest time and in the most interesting manner. The model pupil was the one who could listen longest and remember best what he heard. Good pupils were those who, while in school, could seem dead in all powers save hearing, remembering, and repeating what was told them by their teacher. They had to keep their eyes open, too, not that they were required to see much, but as an evidence that they were awake. Bad pupils were those who were alive beyond the prescribed limit, and those most fully alive were considered the most rebellious and least hopeful pupils. When books were used, the pupils were expected to memorize the words in their text-books as answers to questions set by their teachers. No change was made in the form of the question and no variation allowed in the words of the answer. The comprehension of the meaning of the answers and the relationship to knowledge already in the mind often received little consideration.

In active receptivity the pupil became an independent accumulator of knowledge. He was trained to investigate for himself. He dealt with things as well as words. When he used books for the purpose of study he was emancipated from the slavery of memorizing and repeating the exact words of the text-book, and trained to search for truth as recorded by the wisest of his predecessors.

In passive reflection the pupils were led by their teachers through the steps of logical processes, but they were not trained to think independently. It gradually became clear that "allowing other people's thoughts to run through our minds" is not really thinking, and that such a process weakens originality and tends to make men subservient to existing conditions as established by custom and conventionality.

Active reflection trained pupils to think independently and to respect their own opinions. This step was a great advance in intellectual training and toward the complete liberty of the race.

A still greater advance was made when educators began to realize that knowledge and intellectual power are of value only as they are used, and that the ability to use knowledge and apply power may be trained, and must be trained, if trained at all, by being exercised. This soon revealed the important truth that the training of the executive powers is the only certain method of storing the mind with clearly related knowledge and giving the power to think definitely. Receptive power, reflective power, and executive power form a sequence, which should be developed as a unity. The lower steps of the sequence are not complete in themselves. They find their logical completion in the highest step, and therefore they can reach their true culture only in direct relation to and connection with that step.

But even in the training of the executive powers the domination of the teacher retained its blighting influence until the time of Froebel. Montaigne and

Rousseau had seen the evil influence of adult interference or overshadowing, and had dimly outlined the need of freedom for true individual growth by individual activity. Froebel grasped this germ of thought in its fulness, and made it the fundamental principle underlying the practical methods of his system. He made a vital distinction between activity and self-activity, between expression and self-expression. There is more difference between the results of passivity and self-activity on the part of the pupils in the training of the executive powers than in the culture of the receptive or reflective powers. The higher the educational process, the weaker does passivity appear, and the more limitless do the possibilities of activities become.

The old educational processes are largely responsible for the fact that there are so many men like Mr. Leigh described by Canon Kingsley as one of those men "who possess almost every gift except the gift of the power to use them." Every so-called educated man who fails to use his powers wisely and fully, because his selfhood has not been revealed to him and trained to perform its proper function by directing his energies independently, is an unripe apple falling to set educational Newtons thinking.

Every child has individual power. This power is intended to guide the child's energies. It does guide them until the child is weakened by misdirection or by the substitution of the teacher's authority as a motive power stimulating the child's action. Then selfhood gradually weakens from lack of opportunity for exercise, and the child becomes listless and indifferent. An indolent child is an unnatural child. Children are made indolent by failure to develop their motive character power. Energetic effort at productive work gives them pleasure when it possesses the elements of self-stimulation and self-direction. The child's powers of self-stimulation and self-direction are dwarfed by lack of opportunity for activity, and in such conditions the child ultimately becomes inert, and acts mainly in response to external stimulus. There is little use in training the child's receptive powers or its reflective powers unless its personality is trained at the same time to set them in motion and guide them aright.

Power is given to man that it may be used in co-operation with God. Power so used always increases. The highest ideal of human duty is co-operation with Divinity. The grandest conception of human destiny is growth toward the Divine, and destiny is reached through duty. The truest conception of duty is action for truth and justice in which the inception as well as the execution of the act bears the stamp of individuality. Co-operation means more than acting in concert in obedience to a single leader. The perfect co-operation is that in which each individual has a common purpose, toward the accomplishment of which he works as a free man. Mankind should be co-operatively, independently self-active. Froebel did not aim to make the masses mere followers of a few leaders. He believed in a democracy in which every man was really free and progressively strong and true. Such a democratic brotherhood he hoped to form out of the whole of the human race by universal conformity to the principles of his educational system.

Froebel regarded as one of the chief weaknesses of

humanity the lack of harmony between its powers of insight and attainment. Men know better than they do, and this necessarily leads to moral deterioration. The consciousness of neglect to perform duty as we conceive it produces the humiliation that leads to enfeeblement of character. It is a serious mistake to give a child more power to think without giving it at the same time a correspondingly increased power and tendency to execute its good decisions. The child should be in harmony with himself. The desire of accomplishment should follow naturally as the result of the power to conceive. This essential harmony between insight and the desire for attainment is greatest in young children. That this should be so is not creditable to teachers. Greater power to do should not destroy the tendency to do. Froebel maintained that the desire to accomplish will increase with the ability to accomplish when the pupil is trained in accordance with his law of self-activity. Clearness of conception, definiteness of altruistic purpose, and success in its achievement he regarded as essential steps in universal human happiness.

> "The only rest
> Is labour for a worthy end."

> "He is crowned with all achieving
> Who perceives and then performs."

Whenever the teacher gives the child additional knowledge without at the same time increasing its executive force and tendency, he is helping to destroy the harmony that should exist between its receptive, reflective, and executive powers. Froebel's law of self-activity requires complete unity between the three classes of powers.

Froebel recognised the value of play for many reasons, but no other reason had so much weight with him in leading him to determine to make play an organic part of his educational work as the fact that in play the child's activities are put forth energetically in response to its own personal decision. In play the child is perfectly self-active. In play alone is the child developed as a unity, physically, intellectually, and morally. The whole being then acts in harmony with motives originating in the child's own mind, and free play is therefore a perfect type of true self-activity.

Without self-activity the fullest cerebral growth is not possible, and the co-ordination of the different departments of the brain does not become complete. The free self-activity of the country child gives it, as a rule, a more energetic and better co-ordinated brain than the city child. The country child usually has much greater freedom than the city child, and a much wider and more stimulating range of objective life and experiences. The city child is restrained by conventionalities, and limited by the circumstances of city life. The country child has few conventional restrictions, and usually has the complete equipment of Nature's storehouse to lead him on day by day in a continuous series of interesting investigations and experiments. This is ideal self-activity. No adult accompanies it to suggest the problems it is to investigate. No intermeddling senior says, "See, see!" and thus seals its eyes or trains them to open at the dictation of others. It sees and hears and examines the things appropriate to its stage of development and to its selfhood. Its every act proceeds from selfhood, and therefore reacts on selfhood to produce a greater selfhood. This free self-activity, under proper conditions, produces in the country child a stronger, more vigorous, and better co-ordinated brain than it could have developed under less favourable conditions. If children were compelled to submit to the conditions and processes of most schools during the whole of their waking hours for the first twenty years of their lives, their physical, mental, and moral development would be stunted. The race has been saved by the shortness of the school hours and the persistent recuperative elasticity of the individuality of childhood. Froebel would make the school hours as productive of self-determination as any other part of the day by bringing into schools the fullest opportunities for the interested, energetic self-activity of each child. He rejected the theory that mind storing and the training of the reasoning powers necessitated the obscuring of selfhood, and taught that self-expression is the most effective way of enlarging and storing the mind, of training the reasoning powers, and of defining the personality.

Froebel believed that the true process in the evolution of life is "from life, through life, to life." He saw this process in plant life, from inner life, through functional life, to perfection of the characteristic life of the plant. In the human being he saw the corresponding process from inner life (individuality or selfhood), through the life of self-activity to the perfect life of a harmonious and balanced individuality. He says: "O man, who roamest through garden and field, through meadow and grove, why dost thou close thy mind to the silent teaching of Nature? Behold even the weed, which, grown up amid hindrances and constraint, *scarcely yields an indication of inner law!* behold it in Nature in field or garden, and see *how perfectly it conforms to law!* What a pure inner life it shows, harmonious in all parts and features—a beautiful sun, a radiant star, it has burst from the earth! Thus, O parents, could your children, on whom you force in tender years forms and aims against their nature, and who *therefore* walk with you in morbid and unnatural deformity—thus could your children, too, unfold in beauty and develop in all-sided harmony!"

Froebel demanded that the child be self-active in school, in order that it might reveal itself fully in its greatest powers to its teacher and, what is of still greater importance, to itself. Self-revelation is one of the most important departments of training. Few, very few adults are conscious of their own highest powers. Among the thousands of teachers who have applied to me for positions I have not found one who could definitely answer the question, "What is your greatest power?" Free self-activity is the only way in which self-revelation can be made complete.

Self-activity, doing in response to the child's own originating mental activity, reveals the extent of the child's knowledge as well as its powers, and is the surest way of making knowledge clear to the child's own mind, and of establishing the relationships of varied kinds of knowledge.

Self-activity is the highest method of developing the executive power of the hands in response to the direction of the child's mind. Responsive activity alone develops the motor brain to a limited extent; but such activity does not secure the essential co-ordination between the sensor and the motor brain. It is very important to have a well-developed sensor brain and a well-developed motor brain, but the perfect co-ordination of the sensor with the motor brain is the most important element in brain development. The perfectly trained individual is the one who has physical organs trained to their fullest limit in power and skill to respond definitely and promptly to the suggestions of a well-developed brain in which the sensor and motor elements are balanced and perfectly co-ordinated. No other process but self-activity can produce such mental and physical development and co-ordination, and make each individual self-directing in originating motive and in executive effort.

A very distinct advantage of education by self-activity is the strengthening of the power of self-education. The lack of energetic tendency toward persistent self-education after the period of school life has passed is the most manifest weakness in the influence of educational forces. That this weakness exists should not cause surprise. It would be surprising if any other result were produced by a system of education that makes the pupil dependent on the teacher for the stimulus to study—usually a coercive stimulus—and fails to develop the power of choice on the part of the pupils in regard to certain departments of study. If a boy's selfhood has not been trained to act with spontaneity in regard to study before he leaves school, it is unreasonable to expect it to act with much energy when school life is over. It would be very remarkable if an *internal* stimulus did control him when his teacher had deliberately trained him through his formative years to respond only to *external* stimulus. It is doubtful whether two per cent of all who pass through the public schools persistently and systematically follow any definite course of study after they leave school. Only a small proportion of professional men regularly study the new developments even in connection with their own profession. The schools prevent the development of the habit of independent study by failing to make provision for the exercise of self-activity in study during the formative years of childhood. Pupils who throughout their school life study only in response to the dictation or compulsion of their teachers naturally stop studying when they leave school. Their own motive power of self-acting interest has not been developed, and they have lost the external power that impelled them to study.

A few quotations from Froebel's writings will help to make clear his own conception of the law of self-activity and its paramount importance as a fundamental principle in educational practice.

He wrote with some bitterness of the opposition of the German Government to his system because it tended to give men new conceptions of freedom:

"As a state machine I should have been engaged in *cutting out and modelling* other state machines. But I —I only wanted to train up *free, thinking, independent men.*"

"In order, therefore, to impart true, genuine firmness to the natural will activity of the boy, all the activities of the boy—his entire will—*should proceed from* and have reference to the development, cultivation, and representation of the *internal*."

"As the plant grows through *its own vital power*, so also must human power become great through its own exercise and effort."

"Man is developed and cultured toward the fulfilment of his destiny and mission, and is to be valued even in boyhood, not only by what he receives and absorbs from without, but much more by what he *puts out and unfolds from himself*. Experience, and history too, teach that men truly and effectively promote human welfare much more by what they put forth from themselves than by what they have acquired. Every one knows that those who truly teach gain steadily in knowledge and insight; similarly, every one knows, for Nature herself teaches this, that the use of a force enhances and intensifies the force. Again, to learn a thing *in life and through doing* is much more developing, cultivating, and strengthening than to learn it merely through the verbal communication of ideas."

"The purpose of teaching and instruction is to bring *out* of man rather than to put more and more *into* him; for that which we can get *into* man we already know and possess as the property of mankind, and every one, simply because he is a human being, will unfold and develop it out of himself in accordance with the laws of mankind. On the other hand, what yet is to come *out* of mankind, what human nature is yet to develop, that we do not yet know—that is not yet the property of mankind; and still, human nature, like the Spirit of God, is *ever unfolding its inner essence*."

"However clearly this might and should appear from the observation of our own and all other life, even the best among us, like plants near a calcareous spring, are so incrusted with extraneous prejudices and opinions that only with the greatest effort and self-constraint we give even limited heed to the better view. Let us confess at least that when, with the best intentions toward our children, we speak of their development and education, we should rather say *en*velopment and *in*ducation; that we should not even speak of culture, which implies the development of the mind, of the will of man, but rather of *stamping* and *moulding*, however proudly we may claim to have passed beyond these mind-killing practices."

In speaking of one of the occupations used in the kindergarten, he said: "It gives the boy easily and spontaneously, and yet at the same time imperceptibly, precise, clear, and many-sided results due to *his own creative power*."

"We find the human being, even at the earliest stages of boyhood, fitted for the highest and most important concern of mankind, for the fulfilment of his destiny and mission, which *is the representation of the divine nature within him.* To secure for this ability skill and directness, to lift it into full consciousness, and to exalt it into a life of *creative freedom* is the business of the subsequent life of man in successive stages of development and cultivation."

"Training and instruction should rest on the foundation from which proceed all genuine knowledge and all genuine attainments: *on life itself and on creative effort,* on the union and interdependence of *doing and thinking,* representation and knowledge, art and science. They should be based on the pupil's *personal efforts in work and expression,* making these, again, the foundation of all genuine knowledge and culture."

"To stir up, to animate, to awaken, and to strengthen the pleasure and power of the human being to labour uninterruptedly *at his own education,* has become and always remained the fundamental principle and aim of my educational work."

"The time has now arrived when men are coming to the *consciousness of their own being* and of the law which rules them, and according to which they are active, therefore the earliest childhood must be guided according to this law, and at first in the activity of play. Consciousness of the law is only prepared for by action and the application of the law. *Unconsciousness is raised to consciousness chiefly by action.*"

"The will is strengthened only by *voluntary activity.* By striving to create and produce the beautiful and good the feelings are developed, and *by all lawful, thoughtful, free activity* the mind is cultivated. But such activity sets aside all extraneous education, and that outside indoctrinating that is not in unison either with the nature of the child or with his actual state of development, and it puts *self-education* and *self-indoctrinating* in their place."

"Freedom can not be bestowed upon us. God himself can not bestow it upon us, since it must be the product of our moral and intellectual unfettering, which it is possible to attain *only by self-activity.*"

Froebel based all real development on the revelation of the *inner* in the outer. To him the universal law of human growth consciously toward perfection was: Inner growth is the only real growth, the internal dominates the external, and inner growth springs from the reflex action of the inner on the outer, and not from the direct action of the outer on the inner. The inner power increases by its own activity. Education was to him a unity in every respect, and therefore he insisted that increase in knowledge should be accompanied with increase of power of the inner life, of originative as well as executive power. His *doing* was always the result of *seeing*, and his seeing was made clearer through doing.

He believed that the divinity in the child—its individuality, its distinctive characteristic, its originality, its selfhood—is the element of power that should be most definitely trained, because it is the element of most importance to the child and to the race. On its development rested all his hope for the child itself, and for its uplifting influence on its fellow-men. Therefore he made its training the central element in his system. Self-activity as a law means the definite training of the individuality, the originality, the distinctive characteristics, the selfhood, by calling it into energetic activity in a natural way through spontaneity of interest.

By making the training of selfhood the central element in educational effort he had no intention to neglect the training of the receptive and reflective powers and the communication of wide and thorough knowledge. He believed that the education of the child should be carried on as a unity, and that unless the highest human power was definitely trained no other power could be developed to its fullest limit, nor could the mind be properly stored with knowledge. The highest act in the educational sequence includes the operation of all related, subordinate activity. He objected to every system that magnified knowledge at the expense of the child, and his whole life was a protest against the "stamping and moulding" processes of teachers, who failed to recognise the sacredness of the child's individuality. What he valued was not power, but creative power. He aimed to make something better of his pupils than mere "machines," and, as he so well said, to make them "free, thinking, independent men," always keeping in mind the germ thought that "the fulfilment of man's destiny is the representation of the divine nature within him." This ideal made creative freedom a logical conception. Without it creative freedom would lose its educational value; the suggestion of creative power to human beings would be absurd, and spontaneity might lead to anarchy instead of harmonious growth toward truth, justice, and perfect freedom. He knew that harmonious growth did not require the sacrifice of individuality. His conception of unity was not homogeneity, but an organic unity of dissimilar elements or forces. His theory was unity from diversity, and his aim the reconciliation of opposites. The source of unity and of reconciliation was the vital power of the divine essence in each individual. The more completely he could develop this vital power of selfhood, the more quickly he expected to unite the universal brotherhood of man in a progressive advance. The apparent contradiction between individualism and social unity vanishes as individuals rise to higher ground and broader vision—as their selfhood becomes more fully developed.

The greatest modern educational philosophers of England and America are in harmony with Froebel in regard to self-activity as the basis of growth and real progress.

Sir William Hamilton says: "The primary principle of education is the *determination of the pupil to self-activity,* and that teacher who fully recognises the active agency of the pupil's mind in acquiring knowledge and experience and in applying them to the affairs of everyday life, will be the most useful to his pupils. In the training of youthful minds we regard *formation* as of more importance than *information,* the *manner* in which work is done as of greater consequence than the matter used in the work. All true education is *growth,* and what we grow to be concerns us more than what we live to know."

Herbert Spencer, who is in his philosophy often strikingly like Froebel, says: "In education the *process of self-development* should be encouraged to the fullest extent. Children should be led to make their own investigations and to draw their own inferences. They should be told as little as possible, and induced to discover as much as possible. *Humanity has progressed solely by self-instruction.*"

H. Courthope Bowen writes: "The answer comes from every part of creation with ever-increasing clearness and emphasis—development is produced by exercise of function, use of faculty. . . . To produce development most truly and effectively the exercise must arise from and be sustained by the thing's own activity—its own natural powers, and all of them (as far as these are in any sense connected with the activity proposed) should be awakened and become naturally active."

Prof. John Dewey summarizes the basal principle of all educational method as follows: "The fundamental principle is that the child is always a being with activities of its own, which are present and urgent and do not require to be "induced," "drawn out," or "developed," etc.; that the work of the educator, whether parent or teacher, consists solely in ascertaining, and in connecting with, these activities, furnishing them appropriate opportunities and conditions."

The law of self-activity is now recognised as fundamental by all educational leaders. How can it be made the basis of the general work of the school? The philosophical recognition of the law will do little good unless it is applied. The pupil may be made receptive, reflective, or executive by the life he is compelled to lead in school. If he is made receptive and reflective only, his natural motor character has been weakened. There is a clearly defined tendency in children to execute what they conceive. Expression is the natural result of impression, and the weakening of the character power of the race results from the destruction of spontaneity in the energetic accomplishment of decisions and purposes.

Teachers should test every method and school process which they practise by the attitude of the pupil's selfhood in relation to it. Is the pupil's selfhood passive or active? Is his activity responsive to the suggestion or order of another, or is it the effort to accomplish a purpose originating with himself? Does it result from outer stimulation or inner motive? If action results from outer stimulation, what is the nature of the inducement to activity? Is it mandatory or reasonable? Does the external influence coerce the pupil or simply guide him? Does it develop interest or weaken it? Is it a temporary motive which logically tends to make the pupil self-active and gradually gives place to inner motives and interest that continue the activity spontaneously, or does it leave the pupil inert when the external stimulus is removed? Can activity induced by commands, or by the personal power, will, magnetism, or other influence of the teacher or parent, be made as energetic and as definitely productive as true self-activity, in the acquisition of knowledge, in the development of the brain, both in its motor and its sensor departments, in the co-ordination of these departments of the brain, or in defining the individuality of the child?

If these questions are asked by teachers in regard to the methods of most schoolrooms to-day, candid answers will convince them that the principle of self-activity has yet received but slight recognition. It is only by thus honestly testing their own work that teachers can be aroused to the energetic mental condition that leads to reform and discovery. In revealing the weakness or evil of present methods, and in discovering the new and better way, the central law of teachers should be self-activity.

In all efforts to reform the methods practised in schools it is well to study the processes by which the child develops before it goes to school. This is one of the most important departments of child study. One definite result of such study must be the clear recognition of the natural ability of the child to discover its own problems. Whatever may be its condition in life, whether its environment be the narrow limitations of city life, or the full and stimulating richness of Nature in flower, tree, bird, or insect life, or in the wealth of inanimate material, the child, if it be left to itself, finds problems for the occupation of its mind and hands inexhaustible in number and unfailing in interest. In the discovery and solution of these problems lies the true source of the child's mental growth. No other problems aid in the development of its mind so completely as those discovered by itself.

The power to discover new problems is much higher than the power to solve them. Children are naturally problem finders, the schools make them problem solvers. Before the child goes to school, unless it is dwarfed by the blighting interference of unwise guides, it finds its own problems. It lives in a paradise of wonders and revelations. If brought up in the country, where it is surrounded by myriad forms of living, growing things (birds, bees, beetles, worms, trees, and flowers), and where it has plenty of material (water, sand, stones, and sticks) with which to develop its building, constructive, and transforming instincts, it is occupied during all its working hours in making new discoveries or in performing new experiments. It needs no guide to direct it to the new revelations or to instruct it in making its experiments. The interference of adults destroys the central element of life both in the discovery and the operation.

A very clear distinction should be made between the aid given to children in the solution of problems discovered by themselves and help given in the discovery of problems. Aid in solution may be perfectly proper, because the child's desire to do at first is usually in advance of its power of attainment, and failure to accomplish will lead to discouragement and inertness of character. Help in finding problems makes the child dependent upon others for the perceiving power in seeing new conditions, upon which independent originative power is based.

Originative power is more important than operative power, because it should be the motive to stimulate operative power to action. Without originative motive power operative power is purely mechanical. Both powers should be given opportunities for their fullest development. The one is the complement of the other. Neither can reach its most complete development unless the other progressively develops with it. Operative power should be the expression of the originative power of the individual who operates, and not merely the agency for carrying out the aims or plans of others. The executive power increases in definiteness most naturally through the accomplishment of original purposes and plans. Man should be a creative being. Creative power grows as all other powers grow—by free use. Interference by adults prevents the higher development of the child most completely when it provides a substitute for its creative power, the originating or discovering element in the child's own nature. To arrest the complete development of the power of independent problem recognition weakens the child at the centre of its intellectual nature by checking its natural tendency to self-activity.

The child comes to school from its sphere of independence in problem finding, and is at once set to work at problem solving alone. In every subject the teacher brings the questions and assigns the lessons. The essential unity between insight and accomplishment, between discovery and achievement, between originating and operating, between self-active interest and executive power, between seeing and doing, between problem recognition and problem explanation, is destroyed. The teacher does the important part of the work. The vital and interest-producing part of the process of learning is not performed by the child, and so the child's interest is inevitably weakened. Day by day it becomes less interested, less positive, and more negative. Its nature adapts itself to its new conditions. Its function in school is to solve problems and answer questions, and it soon learns to wait for its problems and questions.

By such teaching the child is made dependent on the teacher in the most essential department of its intellectual power. The highest success in life can not be achieved by solving the problems of life that are forced upon us by circumstances. Man should be more than a conqueror of conditions that thrust themselves in his pathway. He should be able to choose his pathway. He should have power to see new pathways that lead to higher life work. The men who have lifted their fellow-men to better conditions, either physically, intellectually, or morally, have been those who saw new problems of life and helped to find their solution. Few great discoveries have been the result of accidents. They have been made by men who had power to see new relationships between scientific forces already understood or to recognise unexplained problems as evidences of yet unknown forces. Every man should be a discoverer within his own sphere. Every man would possess independent power of discovery if his natural wonder power had been developed properly. It is not possible to give all men equal power to discover new forces or new relationships. As the power to see new problems is the highest intellectual power, it admits of a wider range of development than any other intellectual power, and there must naturally be great diversity between its highest and lowest degrees of development. But every degree of this natural power of problem discovery is capable of culture, and the source of this culture is opportunity for free self-activity.

The natural "wonder power" of childhood should continue through life to be the pioneer element in character, looking ever ahead, around, and upward for new physical, intellectual, and spiritual worlds, to comprehend and to conquer. The curiosity shown by the child in its effort to understand the wonders of the material world and its relationship toward it is its leading intellectual power. It was intended to increase in strength and insight during the child's whole life. The very power that interests the child in the mysteries of the natural world around it, organic and inorganic, should in later years make the mind reach out aggressively in search of the subtler problems of intellectual and spiritual life. We are in touch with an infinite number of unsolved intellectual and spiritual problems of which we are totally unconscious. We might recognise them and aid in their solution. and thereby aid in the conscious progress of the race toward the divine, if our wonder power had been developed fully. It usually dies out from lack of opportunity for exercise.

Mr. McChoakumchild said: "Bring to me yonder child just able to walk and I will engage that it will *never wonder.*" Few deliberately set themselves the melancholy task of the destruction of wonder power, as did Gradgrind and McChoakumchild; but the dwarfing of the power goes on in most homes and schools, and the race in consequence creeps laboriously in the shadow, instead of soaring in ever-brightening light. The power to see new problems should be cultivated more carefully than any other power, because it discovers the most productive fields for the operation of all man's other powers. True self-activity is the only educational process that can fully develop this power.

In arithmetic the pupils are usually asked to solve problems from books or those collected or prepared by their teachers. It is a much more developing exercise to allow pupils to prepare problems than to confine their attention to the solution of problems. Problem making affords wider scope for originality and leads to a more intimate conception of mathematical relationships, numerical combinations, and arithmetical processes than problem solution. The making of a problem involves the logical principles underlying its solution. Pupils are more interested in discovering new problems than in solving those already made. They are more interested in those made by their fellow-pupils than in those prepared by their teachers or found in text-books.

In Euclid, physics, and botany there is a wide field for the development of the problem-finding habit and the cultivation of wonder power.

In history it awakens interest and promotes the fixing of facts in their relationships in the memory, to assign a portion of the subject to be studied with a view to the discovery of the most important events of the period; making it the duty of each pupil to decide what they are, and to prepare a series of questions to be answered by the rest of the class. In this way the searching interest in knowledge is kept alive and developed, each pupil has his conception of historical values broadened and defined, and the history is very thoroughly considered and discussed. The pupil is not a mere gatherer of facts to answer questions assigned by the teacher or to be given at examinations. He is not a passive student following along paths marked out by his teacher; he is an independent searcher viewing historical questions from his own standpoint. Better than all else, he is being trained to study history intelligently after he leaves school. This is really the chief purpose of teaching history. Dr. Arnold said the duty of the teacher in teaching history is to show "that history contains gold, and to train the pupils to dig for it." All pupils can not be trained to dig for historical gold in original sources, but they may be trained to dig in all available sources.

When geography is studied, not as a means of fixing the names and positions of places in the memory, but to learn from the earth the story of its own evolution, and its influence on the development of man, and to understand its relationship to the heavenly bodies around it, no subject affords better opportunities for the culture of the questioning attitude of the mind. Even in the study of literature the mind of the child should be kept independently aggressive in the recognition of the beauty and the profundity of the language and thought.

The questioning, wonder spirit is natural to the child, and, if not destroyed positively and negatively by the schools, it should increase in power and remain a dominant influence in the mental growth of the man. Given full opportunity for exercise in regard to objects and subjects appropriate to the stage of development of the pupil, it will grow rapidly in intensity, power, and range; and led by it the man should have as much enjoyment in dealing with new revelations in the intellectual and spiritual worlds as the child has in solving the wonder problems of the material world.

It is quite true that problem making and questioning by pupils may deteriorate into formalism. All subjects and processes, however great, degenerate in the hands of mechanical teachers. This fact does not prove the inherent weakness of the subjects or the processes.

One of the fundamental reforms most needed in school work is the adaptation of the environment of the child in school to its stage of evolution, so that it may stimulate the child's wonder power and continue its experience as a discoverer of problems, making conscious a higher form of its development before going to school. It is sometimes said that "the duty of the teacher is to set the child going." The child goes before it is sent to school, too often faster than afterward. The teacher's duty is to keep him going as a discoverer and solver of problems and not as a solver only.

The race should be definitely progressive, and each individual should be independently self-progressive.

There must always be leaders—freer, mightier men and women who step out and up in advance of their slower fellows, but all the race should be free and should increase in might. All can not advance at the same rate, but each one should advance by individual effort. Individual effort does not prevent our taking the most complete advantage of the discoveries and accumulated knowledge of others. Every child has for its inheritance the stored knowledge and the developed sovereignty acquired by man over Nature during all the centuries before its birth, but each man and woman should increase the store and extend the sovereignty.

One of Froebel's essential principles of true self-activity is, that the activity must not degenerate into mechanical drudgery. By creative productivity he hoped to make children and grown people happy at work. Work should never be slavery. In the ideal society as he saw it, when humanity becomes truly a unity work will be joyous, productive activity. He would prepare for this condition by making children love work, which to them he made the external manifestation of the inner, creative life. To make a child conscious of its own original power is an important step in its religious evolution. Creative self-activity is a religious exercise, because it lays the foundation for the clear consciousness of unity with God by revealing to the child the fact that it possesses, in however small a degree, one of his attributes.

It is well to point out that Froebel did not intend that free self-activity should mean unrestricted liberty. Freedom within law he regarded as the only true freedom. The gifts, occupations, and even the games in the kindergarten were intended to foreshadow and reveal the great truth, that even creativity must be subject to definite law.

Self-activity should be one of the most important words in a teacher's vocabulary. It should be written on the top of every page of his notebook and printed in letters of gold on the wall of the schoolroom toward which he looks, to keep him in remembrance of its value and of his tendency to overshadow his pupils. Nearly three hundred years ago Comenius announced as one of the great aims of educational progress: "To search out and discover a rule in accordance with which teachers teach less and learners learn more." We are yet striving toward the ideal of Comenius.

Self-expression is infinitely more productive both in acquiring knowledge and in developing power than expression. Accumulation, expression, self-expression, are three advancing stages of educational power. They form a progressive sequence. The highest stage includes the powers of the other two developed to a higher degree of potency as a means of cultivating power or acquiring knowledge. "What man tries to represent or do he begins to understand." "If any man will do his will he shall know of the doctrine." Many emotions, sentiments, and thoughts vanish from our lives "for lack of expression." The effort of self-expression defines the emotions, sentiments, or thoughts, and language forms an objective representation or body for them. The inner life is co-ordinated and classified, emotion and thought are related, and propulsive power is developed by the process of conscious self-expression in any form—language, music, drawing, modelling, or construction. The aroused inner life is worse than wasted if it finds no means for expressing itself in outward form. It leaves in the mind a record for indistinctness and confusion and a habit of inertness, of conceiving without bringing forth, of planning without producing.

Expression in which there is no selfhood leads to enfeeblement of character. The more fully expression is self-revelation the more it develops selfhood and the more it defines and classifies knowledge.

There are two clearly defined though related stages in self-expression: the enrichment and enlargement of the self and its representation. The inner should be increased and improved as well as expressed. Some of Froebel's disciples have exposed Froebel and themselves to ridicule by failing to recognise fully the value of regular additions to the knowledge stored in the mind by the pupils. They do not overestimate self-activity or self-expression, but they do underestimate the enrichment of that which demands expression. Froebel never forgot the increase of knowledge, but he made the child an active agent in the enrichment of its own mind; never a mere passive receiver of knowledge chosen and given by the teacher in content and form.

Each of Froebel's lessons included, so far as possible, the double process of new revelation to the child and of new revelation by the child. Led by the teacher in its earliest efforts, it took the new steps necessary for securing the new element of inner power, either of knowledge or of process; and then it used the new power in unity with the powers previously accumulated to reveal its new and greater self. As the child grows older it does more and more of the accumulation of knowledge and the enrichment of mind independently and needs less guidance as to the character of the new study or work, or the method of using it or doing it. In this way his proper acquisitive attitude toward knowledge is retained through life, and his natural impulse to execute his own plans in an ever-improving self-activity becomes a part of his character.

In all the work of the school the teacher should aim to preserve the true balance between revelation of knowledge and its use in some original form by the pupils. In this way only can knowledge become part of the personal power of the child.

In drawing, for instance, there are really not a great many principles to teach. Skill results from the intelligent practice of these principles. This practice may be imitation or expression. Formerly it was almost exclusively imitation. It should be almost exclusively expression. Expression in drawing represents the child's own conceptions. These conceptions may be objective or subjective. The representation of objective conceptions is now generally practised, but the child is usually restricted to objects selected by the teacher. This develops representative power but not selfhood. Self-activity in object drawing requires the child to choose its objects. By doing so its interest will increase and its special taste develop and reveal itself. There are higher kinds of self-activity in drawing which are rarely practised yet. The representation of imaginative conceptions requires a comprehensive exercise of selfhood, and therefore is more completely self-activity than any other kind of drawing. Imaginative conceptions develop the central power in creativity. The content of the imagination may be designs, plans, or pictures to express ideals or symbolic representations of Nature or human life or any department of the spiritual realm. Self-expression in any of these departments, the expression in design or plan or picture of original conception, is true self-activity, and the teacher's work in drawing is unfinished unless it leads to this. No subject is truly educative till it enlarges or enriches the selfhood.

There should be a great deal of subjective representation by drawing in connection with history, literature, and composition. In history, allegorical pictures may be drawn to represent the course of events, or real pictures may be made as illustrations of events. Occasionally the whole class may be asked to illustrate the same event, but true self-activity leaves each child free to select the most important event, or the one in which it is most interested. In literature the child should express in drawing its conceptions of the most beautiful pen pictures of the authors. As in history, the whole class may be asked to give pictorial form to the same thought. This affords large scope for individuality, but the complete self is not active, unless the selection of the subject to be illustrated is left to the child. The illustration of the pupil's own compositions is a type of perfect self-activity.

The child should be encouraged not only to choose its own objects or subjects in each department of drawing, but also to select with the aid of the teacher's judgment the department in which it has greatest special power.

Composition is the self-active use of the child's language, its power to write, and its knowledge of the subject about which it writes. It also exercises its logical power, and its consciousness of the interrelationship of the parts in a complete whole. It is a pity that the subjects for composition are usually assigned by the teacher. True self-activity requires that the child shall choose its own subject. Then the selfhood originates the process. There is no educational reason requiring that every child should be compelled to write on the same subject. Of course the power to write definitely should be constantly developed by writing answers or opinions in regard to the other subjects on the programme of study or in reporting the results of investigations made by the pupils themselves.

Brief exercises may be properly written in composition to develop power or elegance of expression on the same subject by all the members of a class; but each pupil in writing a regular composition should express the fulness of his mind in regard to a subject which he chooses for himself. Composition is shorn of half its glory unless the pupil believes that he can by writing reveal new thoughts to those who are to hear his composition read. A composition should not merely express what the pupil knows about a subject, it should express thought that he believes to be in some sense of study or original application peculiarly his own. If pupils are defective in power of selection or in the self-faith that gives reverence for their own thought, it clearly proves that their teachers have failed to develop in them the central element of character. Self-faith and self-reverence will develop naturally if afforded opportunities to do so by the employment of the selfhood in originating as well as in operating.

In all other forms of expression the same principles explained in connection with drawing and composition should be carefully carried out. The pupils should express the leading thoughts of their own minds, the clearest pictures in their own imaginations. They are not alike by nature, and the school does a great wrong by every practice that tends to make them alike, and by every method which assumes that they are possessed of exactly the same powers and tendencies. The greater the diversity the more perfect the unity.

It is not enough that pupils should be trained to choose the department of each subject in which they have special power. They should be at liberty to concentrate attention more specifically on the subject in which they have greatest power to excel. This subject or class of subjects represents the selfhood or individuality, and while all subjects of culture and power should be studied faithfully, it should receive special attention, as it undoubtedly indicates the direction in which the individual can do his best work for the race. If voluntary selection is encouraged, voluntary attention will become a vital element in the development of the child, as it will be constantly impelled by active personal interest.

Self-choice should be exercised to a large extent in connection with the study and work to be done by pupils at home. In school, where each teacher usually has a large number of pupils in the same grade, the pupils must necessarily be taught together during the day. This is one of the child's greatest misfortunes. There is no reason for continuing the dwarfing part of the educational process during the evening. If pupils can not choose wisely, or if they do not work at all, except under the compulsion of class standing or some other external stimulus, the teacher's highest duty is to develop in the defective or delinquent pupils the power of choice and the love of work. These are much greater elements in character than accuracy and rapidity in solving mathematical problems, or a memory well stored with facts relating even to the most important subjects. True self-activity in connection with the subject of a pupil's greatest special aptitude is the best correlative agency to form the natural bond of unity between all the subjects of a school course. The outcome of all discussion as to the subject through which all others may be correlated, will be the recognition of the fact that each child can correlate most fully through the subject most directly related to its own greatest power.

Self-activity, including the origination as well as the execution of the motives, was well chosen by Froebel as the fundamental process of his system. It arouses the only perfect interest and attention; it makes the mind aggressively active in regard to new knowledge, and therefore secures the most thorough apperception; it leads to the most complete correlation of the subjects of study; it develops selfhood, and reveals it to both teacher and pupil; it encourages self-faith and self-reverence by giving a consciousness of original, creative power; it makes productive work an expression of joyous gratitude; it is the elemental law of human growth.

CHAPTER V.

PLAY AS AN EDUCATIONAL FACTOR.

IN describing Pestalozzi's school at Yverdun, Froebel says: "I also studied the boys' play, the whole series of games in the open air, and learned to recognise their mighty power to awake and to strengthen the intelligence and the soul as well as the body. In these games and what was connected with them I detected the mainspring of the moral strength which animated the pupils and the young people in the institution. The games, I am now fervently assured, formed a mental bath of extraordinary strengthening power." The value of play as an educational influence became more clear to him year by year until he made it an organic part of his educational system. His views in regard to play may be found in the following quotations from his writings:

"Even if I have brought no new thoughts to the subject, as some will maintain, even if the goal and aim of this education has long been known, *I have given something new in my childish plays*, for they show how we must begin to give activity to the powers of childhood in order that they shall neither rust and be lost for want of use nor overstrained by too early study."

"Child's play strengthens the powers both of the soul and the body provided we know how to make *the first self-occupation* of a child a freely active, that is, a creative or productive one."

"The plays of the child contain the germ of the whole life that is to follow; for the man develops and manifests himself in play, and reveals the noblest aptitudes and the deepest elements of his being."

"Play is the *highest phase of child development*—of human development at this period; for it is self-active representation of the inner from inner necessity and impulse."

"The plays of childhood are *the germinal leaves of all later life;* for the whole man is developed and shown in these, in his tenderest dispositions, in his innermost tendencies."

"It is the sense of sure and reliable power, the sense of its increase both as an individual and as a member of the group, that fills the boy with all-pervading jubilant joy during these games. It is by no means, however, only the physical power that is fed and strengthened in these games; intellectual and moral power, too, is definitely and steadily gained and brought under control. Indeed, a comparison of the relative gains of the mental and of the physical phases would scarcely yield the palm to the body. Justice, moderation, self-control, truthfulness, loyalty, brotherly love, and again strict impartiality—who when he approaches a group of boys engaged in such games could fail to catch the fragrance of these delicious blossomings of the heart and mind, and of a firm will; not to mention the beautiful, though perhaps less fragrant, blossoms of courage, perseverance, resolution, prudence, together with the severe elimination of indolent indulgence?"

These quotations from the writings of Froebel prove that he recognised the value of play as an educational agent more clearly than any other educational reformer. Other writers before his time, especially Plato and Richter, had noted the benefits of play in mind development and character formation as well as in physical training, but Froebel saw its advantages much more clearly than any of them. He revealed to the world the essential function of play in the evolution of the child in every department of its power, and to him alone belongs the credit of making play a definite and important part of the scholastic education of a child. He was not content that any educational force should be left to chance opportunity in securing its proper influence in the development of the race, and therefore he organized play as a vital part of his educational system for the training of young children. If he had done no more for education than this he would have been a great educator. In regard to play, he did for education what the greatest inventors have done for the industrial evolution of humanity. They revealed practical plans for utilizing recognised forces. They deserve the gratitude of the race not because they discovered new forces, but because they made these forces subservient to civilization. Froebel did not discover play as an influence in the evolution of man's physical, intellectual, and spiritual power. He understood its dominant influence on each of these departments of human power more fully than any other educator, but he was not satisfied with clear seeing, nor with giving to his fellows a full exposition of the philosophy of play as revealed to him. He transformed his insight into practical reality, and made play a vital element among the organized educational forces, that should be used in the physical, intellectual, and moral culture of humanity.

The introduction of play as a fundamental element in his kindergarten work made play culture objective, and forced the consideration of its educational value on teachers everywhere. The result of this has been of incalculable benefit in two ways: teachers are awakening to the importance of play as an educational agency, and a truer ideal has been established in regard to the aim of education. The old idea, that the mere storing of the memory was the highest work of the teacher, made it difficult for teachers to believe that any one could seriously suggest that play should be made an organic school process to be systematically carried on as a regular means of educating children. At first the suggestion met with ridicule only; then leading minds acknowledged that play might be of advantage as a rest and a change from severe mental work; next it dawned on a few progressive teachers that play was really better than formal physical exercises for training the child physically in varied activity and in natural gracefulness; until now the world is beginning to understand that Froebel made play an organic part of his educational system not alone for recreation and relaxation, nor for physical culture only, but as the most natural and most effective agency for developing the child's physical, mental, and moral nature, and for revealing and defining its individuality. Play is so entirely different from the old-school processes that the recognition of play as a means of educating children has completely altered the standpoint of educational thinkers, and has done much to free them from the dogma that "knowledge alone is power."

Froebel's work in undertaking to systematize play and direct it so as to make it most effective as an educational force was a difficult and delicate task. He knew that spontaneity must not be sacrificed to system, as the great value of play intellectually and morally depends on the freedom of the child in expressing its own purposes and carrying out its own decisions. It is because play enables the child to act independently within the limits of certain laws, that it is especially valuable as an educational agency. It affords the child the best possible conditions for revealing its inner characteristics in outward form and action, and is therefore the best way to strengthen and define its selfhood. Froebel's task was the systematizing of play under the leadership of adults, without robbing play of its freedom or the child of its perfect spontaneity and independence of action. He knew, however, that reasonable law is the surest foundation for perfect liberty, and that the child loves its plays none the less because they are governed by definite rules, and he took care that so far as possible the kindergartner or teacher should not restrict the freedom or check the spirit of the children. There is no more lifeless exercise than a game played by children when they are not interested in it on their own account. The teacher's part is to suggest a change when joyous interest is beginning to wane, to arouse interest on the part of the unsympathetic, to encourage the timid to undertake new duties and assume new positions, occasionally by skilfully assigning them leaderships which they can assuredly fill successfully, and to applaud the effort to succeed even more than the achievement of success. In all her connection with the playing of childhood the teacher must be governed by a genuine sympathy with child life, and all her suggestions must be given in the spirit of helpfulness, so that no child may ever be conscious of the shadow of interfering domination, which blights its joyousness, checks its freedom, or dwarfs its individuality.

Confining the consideration of the advantages of play to the physical nature only, it is now generally admitted that play gives greater variety of activity and increases the power of the vital life-producing organs more than any formal exercises. No other process can increase lung and circulation power so rapidly and so effectively as running to accomplish a clearly defined purpose in connection with a game or play. Dr. F. A. Schmidt, of Bonn, says: "In the running game lies for the youth a healthy development of the lungs which can not be produced by any other method. Not to give the children the desire to run about freely means that one sins against the health of the rising generation." Dr. Hamilton, after an examination of the British soldiers at Aldershott, in which he found them defective in chest capacity, wrote: "There can be no doubt whatever as to the great benefit of the habit of deep breathing—full inspiration, deep expiration—in ordinary life. Children ought to be regularly trained in this, as under ordinary circumstances at ten years of age they have lost nearly nine inches of chest girth."

The element of joyous interest in play has an important influence on the physical advantages resulting from it. The joyousness is almost, if not quite, as beneficial as the exercise to the health of children. Play is the perfect co-ordination of joy and activity. The activity of play is itself the chief source of joy in the early stage of a child's life. Another decided advantage of play is the fact that the fatigue point is not reached in play as soon as in formal exercises. A boy will run all day without becoming tired, if he is running to accomplish his own purposes in play. The same boy will tire very quickly of formal exercises, although he makes much more energetic efforts in playing than when engaged in the formal exercise.

Froebel was so profoundly impressed by his foundation law of unity or interrelationship that he aimed to develop the whole being of a child by every school process, so far as it is possible to do so. This law of unity made him the prince of correlationists and led him to value play more than formal physical culture, because its good effects are more directly felt in every department of the nature of the child. He did not underestimate the work of formal education either in physical training or any other department of culture, but he insisted on the application of his law of self-activity in physical education as fully as in mental or moral education. He gave direct instruction in all subjects and departments of training in order that the child might have new elements of power to use in expressing its own individuality.

Formal physical culture he did not regard as an end in education any more than the formal teaching of the process of writing or drawing. Writing and drawing he taught, that the pupil might have new methods of self-expression, and so by formal physical training he would define and strengthen the power of the muscles, improve the posture of the body, increase the functional power of the heart, lungs, and other vital organs, and especially remedy any constitutional or hereditary physical defects, in order that the body might become mightier and more perfectly responsive in executing the decisions of the mind in a definite and persistent manner. In physical education, as in all other education, he demanded that the child should originate as well as execute the idea in order to make its effort completely educative, and therefore he advocated play instead of formal physical culture, because interest stimulated effort and action expressed the thought and feeling of the actor. Mr. Bowen says: "Physical exercise should in the main be the expression of ideas and feelings, however simple; and that is why school games, when orderly and free, are found in practice to be of much greater value than school gymnastics, especially such as are merely acrobatic."

Froebel saw the interrelationship between the body and the mind so clearly that he believed the brain itself was largely dependent on the action of the body for its growth. The investigations of physiological psychology have proved his theory to be correct. He gave a new dignity to physical culture by showing it to have an important influence in the development of the brain and the complete co-ordination of the entire neurological system. The whole body in its voluntary and involuntary action is directed by the brain and other parts of the neurological system, and there is no doubt that the body is influenced by the mind; but it is also true that the mind is influenced by the body. They are parts of the same unity and they rise or fall together in physical quality. The interdependence between body and mind is so complete that the body, in its modes of action and even in the form of its executive parts, reveals the character. The unity is so perfect that body and mind react on each other, so that the body not only reveals the mind but helps to form it.

The improvement of the body aids in the development of the brain in many ways. No physical training is worthy of the name of true culture that does not primarily aim to improve the condition and increase the functional power of the vital organs. The brain feels the advantage of better digestion, circulation, and respiration more quickly than any other organ. The quality of the brain's action depends on its organization, but the energy of its action and the length of time during which it can act without fatigue depend on the way it is nourished. Perfect nutrition repairs the waste caused by intellectual effort, and enables the brain to sustain energetic action without loss of renewal power. External stimulus is always dangerous to the brain unless it is well sustained by the internal stimulus of good nutrition. Thousands of teachers still blight the intellects they aim to develop and store by applying external stimuli to overworked and poorly nourished brains. The more earnest and enthusiastic such teachers become the more dangerous they are. The teacher who by his personal enthusiasm spurs tired brains to work beyond the fatigue point is the enemy of his pupils. He weakens them at the centre of their educational power. It is unfortunately true that the weakest and most nervous children are most liable to yield to the inspiration of the teachers whose educational motto is "Bring them on!" The robust boy who plays vigorously and eats well, laughs and sleeps on, indifferent to the urgent appeals of his teacher to work hard at his lessons; the delicate girl whose nervous system is already too sensitive, and whose brain is already too active, is easily led to study too hard and too long. Shattered health and loss of power are usually the result of over-effort on the part of the students whose nervous and nutritive systems are weak. Ambitious parents and "high-pressure" teachers are responsible for many of the ills that increasingly afflict civilized communities.

The difficulty arises from the narrow misconception of what education really means. The general view confines education to the storing and culture of the intellect, and takes no account of the body. From the primary school to the university intellectual tests alone are taken as the standard by which educational progress is measured. The primary pupil is promoted and the university student is graduated on the basis of intellectual accomplishment and the remembrance of his stored knowledge. Teachers and professors ignore the fact that the human being is an organic unity, and that whatever tends to destroy the balance of the individual elements in the unity must be evil in its influence. Many graduates from schools and universities go forth to the battle of life with honors in their hands and weakness in their bodies. They owe both to their school or university training.

The most necessary improvement in scholastic work is

a recognition of the urgent need of bodily training. It is beginning to receive recognition in many schools and some universities, but the recognition so far given is more negative than positive. The body should receive definite, systematic training because it is the executive agent of the mind; because energetic and sustained mental action depends on the support of healthy, well-developed vital organs; because good health is essential to the highest success in the business of life; and because the bodily activities directly influence the development and organization of the brain and the rest of the neurological system. The body deserves the recognition which Froebel gave it, as a part of the interrelated, interdependent unity, man. A man can not be considered properly educated so long as any part of his nature is undeveloped or untrained. No one department of human power can be educated at the expense of another department without injury to the organic whole. This is one of Froebel's fundamental principles, which has so far received only partial recognition. When it is fully understood, physical culture will be more universally adopted as an essential part of scholastic training, and physical development will be taken into consideration in awarding graduation diplomas and degrees. There is as much objection to the course of the college undergraduate who ignores his physical life in a mad strife for what are called scholastic honours as to that of the student who entirely sacrifices mental culture to athletics. The word "scholastic" will yet have a wider meaning, which will include the development of the physical nature as well as the storing of the mind. The schools and universities will soon break the bonds of mediævalism and extend the meaning of terms that have limited the range of vision of educators for centuries. No definition of education now limits its meaning to mind storing, or to mind storing with power to reproduce at examinations what is in the mind; but the schools in giving diplomas, and the universities in granting degrees, still act in conformity with this narrowest of all definitions of education. If on the staff of a university there were one fifth as many professors to train the bodies of students as there are to develop and store their minds, it would be easy to discover a system of ranking students physically on a basis as absolutely fair and just as that now adopted in marking them for their intellectual acquirements. In some way every element that has a dominant influence in deciding a student's fitness for a successful and noble life should be considered by the faculty of his school or university in awarding him a diploma or a degree. The full comprehension of Froebel's law of unity will make clear the duty of all educators to train the body as the agent, and at the same time the developer, of the mind.

The activities of the body have a direct influence on the growth of the brain itself. Physical exercise can not increase the number of cells in the brain, but it does develop cells that without it would have remained dormant or only partially developed. The muscular system of all parts of the body has corresponding brain areas to direct its activities. If even the little finger be not trained to act with as much force, grace, and variety of movement as it is capable of, there is a certain part of the brain that has not reached its highest possible development. Neurologists claim that there is a natural order in which muscular activity should be developed, and that unless the natural order be followed, perfect brain development and complete neurological co-ordination can never be attained. They claim also that school processes in writing, drawing, and other forms of manual work, have violated the natural order of development by training the finger movements before the movements of the shoulder and elbow have been practised sufficiently to develop the parts of the brain corresponding to them, and define the nerve channels which connect them with the brain. Undoubtedly the evil results of this error would be much more clearly seen if pupils were in school all the time, and if their activities were limited to the schoolroom. Fortunately, however, children usually get a fair amount of exercise out of school. If it were not for this fact many of their brain areas would remain undeveloped throughout their lives. Teachers and experimental psychologists have a wide field for research in order to learn not only how writing, drawing, and manual work of all kinds should be taught without changing the proper order of neurological development, but in what order physical exercises should be performed to aid the growth of the brain in conformity with the laws which govern its perfect natural evolution.

Physical activity not only develops the brain itself, it stimulates the growth of the extensions of the cells throughout the nervous system, the neurons and the dendrons, and thus completes the organization of the nervous system with the muscular system. It accomplishes the still higher work of co-ordinating the sensor and motor systems and establishing the necessary definite reactions between the sensor and motor brain areas. Froebel believed that plays were much more effective in the achievement of these purposes than formal physical exercises, because the motor stimulus in executing an independent decision in a game is more definite and more forceful than in carrying out an instruction from a teacher, or imitating a leader; and because while playing the child has to perform such an infinite variety of movements. The unexpected calls to new duties that continually come to each player in a game give the highest opportunities for the perfect coordination of the entire neurological system. The senses must act with accuracy in reporting the exigencies of the game to the brain; the brain must decide promptly the proper course to be taken; the motor system must receive and conduct the message from the brain to the muscles definitely, and the muscles must respond freely and execute the work assigned to them unerringly, if the player is master of the position he fills. Every essential element and condition required to perfectly coordinate the controlling department of a human being is fully supplied by a good game. The ever-varying conditions require alertness of sense, active attention, quick judgment, strong reaction of brain on motor nerves, and perfect responsiveness of muscles. Every part of the delicate machinery of a perfect manhood is called into developing activity by a good game.

One of the chief advantages of all physical culture, and especially of plays, is the training given to the motor system. For centuries the schools have cultivated the sensor at the expense of the motor system. Whether as a result of this one-sided training or not, it is a fact that the sensor system is now stronger than the motor, and there is no danger of developing the motor power and tendency too much. The greatest weakness of humanity is the lack of power, often the lack of reactive tendency, to do as well as it knows; to execute its decisions; to accomplish its designs; to complete its insight in attainment. Most teachers omit executive or motor training, being satisfied with storing the minds of their pupils with the culture products of the ages, and neglecting to use these culture products to stimulate motor or executive reactions in their pupils. Executive tendency is a needed force, and education should develop this tendency in the race. Few of the ordinary school processes require the development of motor reaction. All mere study dwarfs motor power by bringing to the brain new impressions that do not stimulate motor activity. Even such executive subjects as writing and drawing as usually taught do not aid much in establishing executive reaction between the brain and the motor system. The writing and drawing must be self-expression, the manifestation of original thought, in order that the individual shall receive the fullest motor development. All physical training aids in the development of the motor system. However a purpose is formed in the mind, it is immediately carried out in physical exercise. The instruction to perform a certain movement may be given by the teacher's command, or by signal, or by a leader whose actions are to be imitated, but, however it is communicated, it is acted upon as soon as it is received. This must aid in developing the executive tendency in a child, because it helps to form the habit of motor reaction.

Playing is more effective than any other form of physical exercise in developing motor power and tendency. In other forms of physical exercise the mind merely conveys the message of some other person to the motor system. The mind of the individual acting does no original thinking. The activity is the result of a suggestion received from outside the mind. The process is responsive activity instead of true self-activity, and it therefore lacks fulness of educative force, as responsive activity always does, when compared with self-activity. Activity in response to the teacher's command or signal develops a motor character that acts well under the guidance or leadership of another. Such a character makes a useful member of society, but he is not the most perfect character. The aim of education should be to make self-directing men and women with positive characters. There are three types of character: those whose motor systems are not developed, who are trained to receive knowledge and to reflect without acquiring a tendency to execute their decisions; those who are trained to act in response to the suggestions or orders of others; and those who think independently and try to carry out their conclusions. The first character is negative, the second responsively positive, and the third independently positive. The third is the ideal character which the schools should aim to develop. The rapidly changing conditions of a good game, and the complications incident to a keen struggle, afford perfect opportunities for motor development. Commands are sent at the same moment for instantaneous execution to the muscles of the arms, legs, and body, to run, to spring, to catch, to throw, to lean forward, backward, or sideward. The whole body is called upon to perform the most unexpected feats of agility, and to do them promptly and definitely. In the game of lacrosse, for instance, the ball is thrown and the players on both sides start to gain possession of it when it falls. He who exercises best judgment as to the place at which the ball will drop, and whose fleetness is equal to his judgment, secures the ball; but his opponents are within a few feet of him, straining every nerve to reach him before he can deliver it. In a fraction of a second his eye must sweep the field to discover what disposition he should make of the ball. He always has a choice of several plays. It may be best to throw to one of his own side, who is "uncovered" or free in front, or to his right or left, or behind him; or it may be wisest to make a long throw on the flags; or he may decide to "dodge" his opponents by the "over-drop" "or the under-drop," or to pass them by feinting and sweeping past them; but the important educational development results from the fact that his choice must be made in an instant, and his decision executed at once. No other process so completely develops the mastery of the mind over the body and so fully trains the body to respond perfectly to the mind as a good game. The brain, the motor system, and the entire body are co-ordinated in their action, until the expert player performs feats of agility or skill which to the unpractised appear to be almost impossible.

This infinite variety of motion, in which all the muscles of the body are called upon to participate to the fullest extent of their power and activity, gives to play a double value. It gives a symmetrical and comprehensive physical culture, and it calls every part of the motor brain into action and therefore aids in its development.

There are two classes of games that are especially important for young children: the running games and the throwing, bowling, and quoiting games. Running is the great developer of lung power. The heart, too, is strengthened by the increased exercise caused by the greater demands made on it during a running game. Full development of heart and lungs depends largely on the running games of childhood and boyhood. Teachers neglect one of their most important duties if they fail to give specific attention to running games for pupils from seven to twelve years of age. There may be children whose hearts are organically diseased, who may be injured by running exercises continued too long. It is therefore important to guard against overexertion at first.

The throwing, bowling, and quoiting games are of the highest value in co-ordinating the neurological system, and in developing motor control of the muscles of the executive parts of the body in proper order. In all such games the ball or other plaything used is held in the closed hand, and so the fingers are not called into action. The muscles of the shoulders and arms are trained to respond to the decisions of the brain, and in this way the nerve connections are established with these muscles and the proper neurological centres are first defined. It would be well if all children were trained in accuracy of throwing at a target as men are trained to shoot. In bowling every child should be trained to deliver the ball straight at a wicket. Sides may be chosen and each child allowed to deliver the same number of balls at a target or an unguarded wicket; the aim being to see which side can hit the wicket most frequently. It would be an advantage to have children trained to throw, bowl, and pitch with the left as well as the right hand.

The moral effects of play are most important. The play of a boy corresponds to the work of a man. Every quality that is requisite in the man to make him completely and honourably successful is necessary to complete success in the plays of the boy.*

The weakening self-consciousness of childhood, the most restrictive influence in a child's life, is overcome by social intercourse on the playground under the stimulating conditions of co-operative effort to achieve success.

Self-control, positive as well as negative, is acquired by the independent performance of the varied and unexpected duties incident to games, which requires each player not only to restrain but to direct his own powers. Too often the only self-control that is developed in character forming is the restraint of power. Self-direction is the highest self-control.

What splendid opportunities the boy has to develop energy of character! As Froebel says, there is no room for "indolent indulgence" on the playground. The goal can not be reached unless a supreme effort is

---

* The girl should play quite as much as the boy, that the mothers of each succeeding generation may become more physically perfect both in body and brain. Froebel's work is aiding in overcoming the foolish conventionality that objects to allow girls the fullest freedom in play. The same classes of plays are suitable for both girls and boys under thirteen years of age.

made. The ball can not be caught unless he runs at his best speed and finally leaps forward, impelled by the concentrated energy of his whole nature. "Every nerve must be strained" to gain even half an inch in jumping or vaulting. The winning half inch has done much to mould mighty men. Froebel wisely said: "A child that plays thoroughly, with self-active determination, perseveringly, until physical fatigue forbids, will surely be a thorough, determined man, capable of self-sacrifice for the promotion of the welfare of himself and others."

Courage is required in play, especially in football, lacrosse, and other games in which team competes continuously against team for the possession of a ball. There is no use for the coward on the football or lacrosse field. The "scrimmage" calls for as much courage as the field of battle. Personal fear goes out of a boy's life after he has had a few years' experience amid the inspiring struggles incident to outdoor sports. He learns to think only of his predominant aim, and loses his personal, weakening self-consciousness in the desire to achieve the end directly in view. Self is thus subordinated, and the unconscious subordination of self in a purpose is the basis of courage. Courage is not mere spasmodic daring under specially trying circumstances. Courage of the sternest kind is the spirit that enables one to bear defeat bravely, and to persevere hopefully even in the face of defeat or disaster. The boys who after defeat practise faithfully to qualify for future victory are developing true courage, courage based on resolution that will yield to no defeat. Such courage lays the foundation for the perseverance that "removes mountains," and triumphs over life's fiercest opposition.

Self-faith is one of the most essential elements of strong character. The playground is the place where teachers can do most to develop it in their pupils. Step by step a boy can measure his progress among his fellows and relatively compare his strength of to-day with his weakness of last year, and at each step in advance there comes into his life a consciousness of new power. He notes how earnest effort and persistent practice enable him to achieve victory, and each new triumph adds to his faith in himself.

One of the most essential qualifications for good citizenship is reverent submission to law. The boy's first training in obedience to law under the circumstances of full citizenship is obtained on the playground. There he is among his equals, and the rules of the game are the laws by which every player must be governed. The habit of obedience to rules in boyhood is the surest foundation for co-operative submission to laws in manhood. Plato said: "If children are trained to submit to laws in their plays, the love for law enters their souls with the music accompanying their games, never leaves them, and helps them in their development." The ancient Greeks had a clear comprehension of the unity between the body and the mind, and of the intellectual and moral advantages of physical training.

On the playground, too, the boy learns by experience the two greatest lessons of human responsibility and relationships; of individuality and community. The member of a baseball or a cricket club learns that each player has special duties belonging to his position that can be performed by no other player, revealing special power and special responsibility; that unless he does his part faithfully and skilfully his club is weakened; that the more perfectly each individual plays the more successful the club will be; and that, however excellent each individual may be, failure must result unless the club as a whole works as a unity with a single purpose. In all his plays he is a member of a community in which he has to recognise and respect the rights of the other members, and in which he co-operates with his own side for the accomplishment of a definite aim. Thus experience forms in his mind apperceptive centres of individuality and co-operation around which may be grouped in later years the profoundest philosophy of individualism and socialism and their harmonious relationships.

Play and all methods of wise physical culture influence character by making the body more erect and well-poised, and by making its action more definite, more forceful, more graceful, and more free. The improved attitude of the body reacts on the character in two ways: The functions of the vital organs are more fully performed, because they are more free, and character therefore gains in force; and the consciousness of erectness and poise brings with it an added consciousness of self-faith, dignity, and integrity. The body becomes in time an external manifestation of the character. The motions of the arms, the step, the habitual attitude, the poise of the head reveal to the experienced observer the character behind them. To a certain extent it is equally true that the body by its attitudes and its modes of action influences the mind. Body and mind are so intimately interrelated that the one necessarily reacts on the other. Make the sweep of the arms more free and the conception of freedom is widened; and the new conception is registered in the brain and nerve centres by changes effected in their development, their structure, or their paths of action to correspond with the new movements they have been required to direct. Change that boy's step from his shuffling gait, and make a definite, free step habitual and you have helped to change his character. That boy whose knees bend weakly as he stands lacks moral fibre as well as physical definiteness. Leave that listless boy in his present condition and he will do little to stir the world around him; but by the persistent use of attractive plays and other wise physical culture give him more power and make energetic motor activity automatic in his life, and he may leave his mark, not on the sands of time only, but on the everlasting rocks of eternity. In all cases transformation of bodily attitude or activity is accompanied by a gradual change in moral quality and force, which is based upon an improved mental quality and mental force that is recorded in the brain and other parts of the neurological system. Thus the body not only reveals the character but helps to form it.

It is true that the spiritual nature controls the physical, but the physical nature also influences the spiritual. It is easier for evil influences to corrupt and destroy the character of young men with weak, untrained, inactive, imperfect bodies than it would be if they had vigorous, well-developed, well-trained bodies. Paradoxical as it may seem, there is much truth and force in Rousseau's epigrammatic statement that, "the weaker the body the more it commands; the stronger it is the more it obeys." There is a direct relationship between moral and physical perfection. The spiritual, the intellectual, and the physical form a closely interrelated unity, each element of which affects and is affected by the others.

Play is of service in preventing periodic attacks of lawlessness in children and young men, which result from overcharging with unused physical vitality. Play gives a natural outlet for the energy, and increases the capacity of the body for energetic action without making it a "storage battery." Energy should be used as it is generated. The storing of energy either of mind or body weakens the power to create energy. Rest is needful, but its benefits result from the restoration of the power to produce energy and not from the accumulation of energy. Unused power is always dangerous, and produces an evil effect which is the opposite of the good it should have accomplished. The aim of the educator should be to develop the power to create energy as it is required for use. A playing school is easily controlled. Wise teachers use play or other forms of physical exercise as one of their best agencies in securing discipline naturally and effectively. It is the surest and quickest way to secure order, system, and co-operation in a disorderly, irregular, and indifferent class.

Play is better than gymnastics or any formal physical exercises, because it is more natural, because it is true self-activity, because it is the child's real work, because the benefits derived from it are incidental and not the direct object of the effort made, and because it develops the entire nature of the child at the same time.

Play is natural. The universal tendency of healthy children is to play, and this love for play was given because energetic effort is essential to the fullest growth of a human being, not only physically, but intellectually and morally.

Play is true self-activity, because the child's actions in playing are the result of its own decisions in response to its own motives for the accomplishment of definite purposes in connection with the game, and not in response to the teacher's command or signal.

Play is the child's real work. Some educators hesitate to admit the wisdom of a system of education which makes play an important element in the child's development even in its early years, fearing that the love of play may prevent the love of work afterward. But play is the real work of childhood, and the love of play in the child should become the love of work in the man. Every characteristic of excellence in playing—quickness, alertness, enthusiasm, persistence, energy, and independence—is a characteristic of a good worker at maturity.

Play is the only complete means of self-expression the child possesses. It is the agency by which it defines and strengthens its powers and learns to use them intelligently as a self-directing, self-revealing being in the accomplishment of its own aims. Active physical play is but one department of the child's play life. It very early shows a tendency to play with the material things around it. It is filled with a passionate desire to modify the conditions of things. Unfortunately, most of us lose this aggressive attitude which is the foundation of all progress as we grow older, and passively accept conventional conditions as we find them. The very same tendency that too often makes a child destructive in its play should make it constructive and self-reliant. Play with material things is the highest possible means for making an original and intelligent worker, and outdoor games and sports are the best agencies for developing physical power and the concentration of energy for the achievement of clearly defined purposes.

The benefits of play are incidental. This is a most important advantage. Incidental results are most lasting in all educational work. The unconscious tuition of life and school is the best. The teacher whose ideal is highest and whose art is most perfect values least the direct results of his teaching. The man who takes exercise for the benefit of his health never improves so much as the man who takes the same exercise for some other purpose. The old-fashioned doctor said to his patient, whose system needed the toning of invigorating exercise, "Take a walk of four miles every morning before breakfast"; or "Ride for an hour every morning"; or "Buy a pair of clubs and swing them." The wise physician learns the tendencies of his patient and gets him interested in some work or game which involves the necessary exercise in the accomplishment of some ardent desire. He leads him to take an interest in gardening, or botanizing, or boating, or lacrosse, or tennis, or baseball, or cricket, or curling, or skating, or cycling, for the interest or pleasure connected with the work or the game. Yonder are two men walking toward a high hill. One is a dyspeptic ordered by his doctor to take exercise for his health, the other is on his way to visit the woman of his choice. The glories of the hour in sky, meadow, bird song, flower, and landscape unconsciously fill the soul of one with irritation and the other with exhilaration. The first on reaching the foot of the hill looks despairingly up, and turns back with the feeling that he is too weak to climb the hill to-day, thus losing the part of the walk that would have done him most good. The second goes bounding up the hill confident that just beyond its brow she who is all of life to him will be watching for him, and waiting to welcome him. To the first the physical exercise of walking is drudgery; to the second it means joy and life.

But the highest educational value of play rests on its influence in developing the selfhood of the child, and on its beneficial effects in the training of the physical, intellectual, and moral natures.

Froebel regarded play as the child's natural preparation for work in maturity; as its best means for developing its physical, intellectual, and moral powers; as its chief source of joy; as its highest means of self-expression and self-revelation; as a safeguard against the indulgence of destructive desires and mere sensual pleasures. He considered play a kind of religious exercise for children. A lady who was visiting his kindergarten said after seeing the children at their play: "It seems as if I were in church, it sounds so devotional." Froebel replied: "That is the uniting power of play, which blesses and exalts children and even grown-up people." Middendorff, one of his life-long associates, and the man who was most fully in sympathy with him, caught his reverent spirit in regard to play, when he said: "This is like a fresh bath for the human soul when we dare to be children again with children."

The plays of childhood satisfy two desires of all

healthy children—the longing for activity and for joy. Activity and joy are very important elements in true religion. Perfect soul growth in childhood is the only sure foundation for perfect soul development in maturity, and the child soul gains strength chiefly through joyous activity, therefore Froebel longed to increase the play sphere of childhood, and give all children the fullest opportunities for the joy, the activity, the self-expression, the mind culture, and the moral development of play.

The influence of Froebel's course in making play a part of his educational system has been felt in every part of the world. The German people have been convinced that formal physical culture in school and gymnasiums will not develop a strong and enduring race. The greatest educational advance made in Germany during the closing decade of the nineteenth century is the movement conducted by the educational department of Prussia in favour of public playgrounds. Froebel's educational play system is producing a deep impression in his native land. It has made the Prussian Government do what Dr. Wiese, in his German Letters on English Education, published in 1877, declared to be quite impracticable. In speaking of English schoolboys he said: "Most of them, with the fresh colour of health on their countenances, their bright eyes, firm gait, without a trace of constrained behaviour, were to me often a refreshing picture of blooming youth." He proceeds to describe the causes that have produced such a grand result, and says: "As among these causes, physical exercises and games, such as cricket and others, which aim at adroitness and strength of body, occupy a prominent place among the customary means of education, one might perhaps think of transplanting such things into Germany. The wish that this might be done has been expressed to me during my present stay in England by Germans who were able to compare the two countries in regard to the physical training of youth; and, in fact, German teachers have repeatedly agreed to study these games in England in order to introduce them among themselves. The attempts have been made in vain. The conditions of life are too different in the two countries, and we shall never be able to make up our minds to devote as much of the time of our school hours as seems requisite for games which, after all, would not be a proper substitute for gymnastic exercises."

Dr. Wiese made two mistakes. He ventured to restrict the development of the future. He asserted that the Germans "would never make up their minds to devote much time to games"; and in fourteen years the Germans did exactly what he said they never would do. The grandest achievements of the race are those that have been proved impossible. He erred also in assuming that games should be considered a substitute for gymnastic exercises. The one should be the complement of the other; neither can be a substitute for the other. The leaders in athletic sports are usually most active in gymnastic practices. The general introduction of plays into Germany has increased the attendance in the gymnasiums.

Outside of Germany play education has awakened a deeper interest in physical education and broadened educational ideals generally. It has aided especially in the comprehension of the interrelated unity of the physical, intellectual, and spiritual natures, and this is revealing two great principles. First, the threefold nature should be trained as a unity, as no department can reach its fullest perfection without the adequate development of the other two. Second, the weakest department of a child's nature requires most careful training and nurture. This is especially truc when the physical nature is weakest. Dickens taught the world many educational lessons in his own inimitable way. One of the most valuable of these was the lesson taught by the disastrous results that followed the irrational cramming of Paul Dombey. Paul was killed by his father and Dr. Blimber. His aunt, Mrs. Chick, told his father that "Our darling is not altogether so strong as we could wish. The fact is, his mind is too much for him. His soul is a great deal too large for his frame." Notwithstanding these facts Mr. Dombey took Paul to Dr. Blimber's school and gave instructions that he was to learn "everything." Dr. Blimber accepted the commission, ordered Miss Cornelia "to bring Dombey on," and his mind and spirit, already too strong for his weak body, were strained to their utmost limit. His feeble, overtaxed body soon yielded to the strain, and his premature death resulted from the ambition of his father and the ignorance of his highly learned teacher. Learned he was in the "deceased languages," but completely ignorant of the most important educational principle, that the human being is an organic unity of interdependent elements. Paul's mind and spirit were relatively too active for his body, yet no attempt was made to develop his body. The departments of power already too active were wrought at high pressure; the weakest department was utterly neglected and robbed of its share of nutrition by keeping the brain in an abnormally active condition, while the body had no opportunity for the increasingly energetic exercise so essential for its proper development. The law to determine the amount of special culture for the individual elements of power in human character should be: give most careful culture to the weakest element.

There is an inviting field for teachers in the work of improving the plays of children. The best teachers and the wisest physicians and neurologists will yet devise new games to accomplish specific aims in the development of childhood. So important an agency in the evolution of the race should not be left to chance. Froebel's organization of children's plays was the work of a master genius. With wondrous skill he arranged a comprehensive system of games that call into play the physical and mental powers, strengthening, defining, and co-ordinating them; that give the child the first steps in manual training, and the control of the material world for the purposes of utility and beauty; that reveal the family and social relationships in the home and society; that awaken a sympathetic interest in the work of the labourers in the industrial world; that develop the child's energy, courage, self-faith, and executive power; that make him conscious of individual power which he delights to use creatively, and which, he also learns through play, is given to him that he may use it to make the organic unity of the race more perfect; that appeal to the æsthetic nature by the production of beautiful forms and by the accompaniment of music in time with which the games are played; that introduce the child to Nature and through Nature to the unseen forces behind and within Nature; and that symbolize the work of a perfect life. Yet, perfect as Froebel's system of plays already is, there is a need for an evolution in games in connection with actual school work, and under the direct control of teachers and pedagogical neurologists after school hours. In some respects the most remarkable evolution of modern civilization is the enormous increase in the percentage of the population of civilized countries who reside in cities. The children of the cities lack many of the opportunities for physical, intellectual, and moral growth enjoyed by the children of the country. One of the greatest needs of city children is opportunity for free, energetic playing. Scientific, educational, Christian philanthropy has no better field of operation than in providing ample playgrounds in cities, and in equipping them with the necessary materials for playing the most developing games. The child of the fourth generation brought up in a large city is a pathetic study. It is one of the saddest sights in the world, because it is almost without the instinct of play. Slavery left behind it the evidence of its terrible nature in a race of children who do not know how to play, from whom the tendency to play has been almost eliminated. Rev. William Gillies, the veteran educator of Jamaica, reports that "one of the greatest difficulties to be overcome in the physical, intellectual, and moral evolution of the negro race in Jamaica is the fact that the children have lost the play spirit." This is a most interesting and suggestive fact to teachers.

The recent German playground movement should become universal. Froebel's appeal to fathers and mothers may be adopted with profit by the teachers and philanthropists of the world: "Play is not trivial; it is highly serious and of deep significance. Cultivate and foster it, O mother; protect and guide it, O father! To the calm, keen vision of one who truly knows human nature, the spontaneous play of the child discloses the future inner life of the man." As Schiller said:

"Deep meaning oft lies hid in childish play."

CHAPTER VI.

THE HARMONY BETWEEN CONTROL AND SPONTANEITY.

As Froebel's fundamental law is unity, and his fundamental process is self-activity, so his fundamental principle in discipline is the harmony between control and spontaneity. This principle is based on his law of harmony of opposites.

Dr. Harris says: "Careful students of the history of education have noticed the fact that its reforms swing from extreme to extreme. At one time it will become the fashion to lay great stress on the training of the will. Schools will accordingly become places where children are submitted to semi-mechanical processes of discipline to the neglect of individual insight and ability to think. Gradually the pendulum will swing to the other extreme, and discipline will be neglected for the intellectual self-activity of the pupils.

"The intellect grows by mastering for itself the thoughts of others, and by investigating causes and principles. But the will grows through self-sacrifice for the sake of wider and wider interests. It is possible, therefore, to have two lines of educational reform antagonistic each to the other."

Froebel was the first educator to see the perfect unity

between these two lines of educational reform, and to harmonize control and spontaneity, direction and freedom. In doing so he claimed to secure more perfect development of both than had been achieved before. He saw the tendency "to swing from extreme to extreme," and he knew that it was caused by the principle of separation or atomism, or extreme individualization. With wider intellectual vision he discovered the law of unity, and saw the philosophical oneness of apparent opposites.

Froebel's views on this question may be gathered from the following extracts from his writings:

"Education in training and in all instruction should be by far more *passive and following* than categorical and prescriptive; for, by the full application of the latter mode of education, we should wholly lose the pure, the sure, and steady progressive development of mankind—i. e., the free and spontaneous representation of the divine in man, and through the life of man, which, as we have seen, is the ultimate aim and object of all education, as well as the ultimate destiny of man."

"In accordance with the laws of Divine influence, and in view of the original soundness and wholeness of man, all arbitrary (active), prescriptive, and categorical, interfering education in the forms of instruction and training must of necessity annihilate, hinder, and destroy."

"Therefore education as instruction and training, originally and in its first principles should necessarily be *passive, following* (only guarding and protecting), *not prescriptive,* categorical, or interfering."

The words "passive" and "following" in the preceding quotations refer to the teacher, not to the child.

The child should be the active agent in its own education. Froebel had such unbounded faith in the right tendency of humanity, and such abhorrence of the idea of the "total depravity" of childhood, that he taught in all his works that the teacher's duty is to place the child in proper conditions, and supply it with material adapted to its stage of development. Having done these things, he should reverently "stand from between the child and God," and watch it grow, using his developed wisdom to study each individual child and adapt special conditions to guard it from evil and stimulate its best and fullest growth. These quotations relate to the training of children whose inner life is not warped. He knew that conditions must be met as they exist. He saw the possibility of the need of prescription, but taught that "all prescription should be adapted to the pupil's nature and needs, and should secure his co-operation. This is the case when all education in instruction and training, in spite of its necessarily categorical character, bears in all details and ramifications the irrefutable and irresistible impress that the one who makes the demand is himself strictly and unavoidably subject to an eternally ruling law, to an unavoidable eternal necessity, and that, therefore, all despotism is banished."

"Between educator and pupil, between request and obedience, there should invisibly rule a third something to which educator and pupil are equally subject. This third something is the *right*, the *best*, necessarily conditioned and expressed without arbitrariness in the circumstances. The calm recognition, the clear knowledge, and the serene, cheerful obedience to the rule of this third something is the particular feature that should be constantly and clearly manifest in the bearing and the conduct of the educator and teacher, and often firmly and sternly emphasized by him."

The fact that he recognises the need of categorical teaching and training, and the firm and stern emphasis of justice, does not contradict the theory previously quoted, which presents the ideal education for children without defined evil in their natures.

"The kindergarten is the free republic of childhood."

"The aim of my kindergarten is to prevent the children of the masses from growing up like little savages, and also to save the schools from a lawlessness which is miscalled liberty."

"If national order is to be recognised in later years as a benefit, childhood must first be accustomed to law and order, *and therein find the means of freedom.*"

His great interpreter, the Baroness von Marenholz-Bülow, brings out prominently this phase of his teaching. She says:

"Nothing is left, then, but to set *free* obedience in the place of *blind* obedience, and to render the masses through cultivation capable of seeing that only the self-restraint of individuals and their voluntary subjection to law make greater freedom in society possible. That mode of education which can solve this problem may justly be called education for freedom."

"Certainly the application of a given rule or law must, by the formative and creative productiveness of the kindergarten pupils, awaken their sense of law and order, and call forth the beginning of an opposition to all disorderly and anarchical action."

"Froebel's system aims to smooth the path for the future free and conscious obedience to law, and thereby lead at the same time to the highest possible degree of freedom.

"By means of kindergartens a place of education is created which represents a miniature state for children, in which the young citizen can learn to move freely, but with consideration for his little fellows."

The aim of Froebel was to make the school the "free republic of childhood," in which the child should be a self-active agent, guided by a teacher wise enough to direct it without making it conscious of interference, and to place it in conditions to define its recognition of law, and at the same time give ample scope for its originality. There may be life under law or deadness under law. Froebel wished to have law always and everywhere, but with it he demanded the right of the child to free life, positiveness, and self-direction, instead of coercion, negativeness, and mechanical following. He reverenced the individuality of the child, and he knew that spontaneity was the only perfect basis for the growth of individuality; he aimed to give individuality the power of self-direction, and therefore he insisted upon freedom of will action as the only foundation for the growth of the will; but he recognised the universality of law, and he made it the duty of the trainers of childhood to reveal law in its beneficence, and not in its enslavement. Like every good, law may be a blessing or an evil. Froebel aimed to make law aid in developing constructiveness instead of destructiveness; in guiding, not merely in restraining. The coercive teacher or parent recognises only the restrictiveness of law. That is its dark side. The highest art of the teacher may be shown in revealing "the perfect law of liberty"; in guiding the child through its years of weakness to complete self-control, so that no step may interfere with the development of selfhood, and yet every step lead to a consciousness of law. The outer control should gradually vanish as the inner develops.

The Scotch lad is usually controlled by his father's iron will. His duty in childhood and youth is unreasoning submission to law. There is power even in such discipline. In the boy's soul dread of parental authority becomes in time a solemn veneration for the majesty of law; and reverent submission to the human father rises into devout subordination to God, and forms the granite in Scotch character individually and nationally. Such training makes men strong, but narrow. It places law above liberty, and recognises the power of the Creator more than his love. It values individual rights more than individual growth. This is control without spontaneity.

In too many homes there is spontaneity without control. The results are usually disastrous. Control alone is better than spontaneity alone for perfecting strength of character; better even for the development of productive spontaneity. Uncontrolled spontaneity would be the ideal educational condition if all natural tendencies were toward truth, or if all children had from their earliest years enlightened consciences, developed wills, and a recognition of the rights of others so clear as to make them unselfish, and so strong as to be a controlling force in their lives.

Control and spontaneity have been regarded as antagonistic forces in the development of the child. They are really twin powers that should work in harmony. Truth can never be at variance with other truth. There are no irreconcilable contradictions, no chasms that clearer insight shall not span. Man can not always see the harmony between principles that appear to be in conflict, but infinite wisdom sees the mutually strengthening interrelationship of apparent contradictions. Nature rejoices in the equipoise of opposing forces. As man grows consciously toward the Divine, he sees harmonies more clearly, and the revelation of new harmonies between the controlling laws of the universe makes the sweetest music that ever lifts his soul to higher joy. After the battles of past ages, the veterans who fought for opposing principles have joined hands in loving unity, when they have climbed through the clouds of error, and clearer, wider vision has dispelled illusions and shown the essential oneness of truths which partial insight had supposed to be at variance. Each party saw a single truth, and in the brighter light on the hilltop the two truths were blended into one.

Rightly understood, control and spontaneity work in perfect harmony. Spontaneity does not mean freedom from law, but freedom through law, in accord with law. Productive spontaneity can not be at variance with law; it can exist only in conformity with law. Law and liberty are indissoluble. They are giants whose union produces life and growth. The "law of liberty" is the perfect law. David spoke wisely when he said: "So shall I keep thy law continually for ever and ever, and I will walk at liberty." "To the truly free man, freedom coincides with control." Spontaneity is th- essential condition of individual development; law defines relationship of the individual to the universal; control is the application of law. There is no wrong to the child in the exercise of wise control by parents and teachers. Such control is absolutely essential to the full development of character. We should control childhood in order to define respect for human law and reverence for Divine law. The perfect work of Christianity will be accomplished when all mankind is consciously, reverently, responsively, co-operatively submissive to the Divine will. This condition can never be reached until the child in the home and in the school lives a life of co-operative obedience to its parents and teachers, and is thus qualified for conscious co-operative submission to the authority of the state, and beyond this to a cheerful recognition of Divine authority and the progress resulting from coworking with God.

Children should be controlled because wise and definite control by a superior will develops the will power of the child, and qualifies it to direct its own life when it reaches maturity. If unchecked, the feelings and passions of a child sweep in an unrestrained torrent over its undeveloped will; lack of control becomes habitual; selfishness and self-will act automatically, and character power is lost. More than half the energy of humanity is dissipated. Character energy must be controlled and directed by an enlightened will in order to become an executive force for good. The child's will is neither sufficiently strong nor sufficiently enlightened to guide its activities and control its powers. Uncontrolled forces lead inevitably to ruin and disaster. It is a lamentable fact that so much of Nature's physical force remains yet unmastered, but the saddest sight in the world is an uncontrolled soul.

But, while control by a superior will is essential and natural, it should never prevent the full development of spontaneity of character. It is not necessary to dwarf a soul by controlling it. The child's individuality can not be weakened without fatal consequences. Each child has an individuality of its own. It is a sacred power intended to grow for ever. It is the divine in the child. It can not be marred or misdirected without interfering with God's plan. God's will is never a substitute for man's will; neither should the will of the teacher be in any way a substitute for the will of the child. The teacher's will may direct the child's will, but never safely act in its stead. The teacher's personality should never intervene between the child and the light.

To be truly beneficent, external control must stimulate as well as restrict. It should be exercised with a constant consciousness of the child's selfhood, and in harmony with several clearly defined laws.

Control by external agencies should last for the shortest possible time. Self-direction should be our aim for our pupils from the first.

Human control, like Divine control, should be prompted by love, based on love, and exercised in love. Human love is man's strongest controlling force, as well as his greatest life-giving power. Divine law is often necessarily restrictive of wrong, but it is lovingly restrictive. It is stimulating and growth-giving; never destructive.

Control should never degenerate into coercion. Plato said, "A free mind ought to learn nothing as a slave."

There is no life-giving power in coercion. There is no growth in mere negation. God meant our characters to be positive, not negative. One "do" is worth a thousand "don'ts" in the destruction of evil or the production of good. Coercion may repress evil; it never eradicates it. It can only repress the wrong for a limited time, and in doing so it restricts the good. Coercion never made a child creative, and the growth of creative power is the central element in its education. Coercion does more than restrict the power of a child; it corrupts its ideal. The common and unnatural dread of Divine authority arises from the degradation of human authority into unreasoning, unloving coercion.

The terrorism of the unknown is the most dreadful form of coercion. Attempts to secure passive submission by threats of punishment by the mysterious interference of imaginary monsters have done as much as any other cause to destroy the true spontaneity of childhood. It is impossible to conceive the fulness of the evil influence of such threats at a time when the child's imagination is most active. The imagination itself is perverted, and often becomes a corrupting instead of a purifying power. The child's activity becomes passivity; its instinctive interest in the great unknown dies out, and its spiritual development is thus prevented. The unknown land should be filled with angels, not demons. Many parents and teachers degrade even the Father of light and love into a sort of goblin to terrorize their children. With sacrilegious impudence they dare to say to children, "God won't love you if you are bad," till the child gets its little heart filled with misconceptions of God and irreverence for him, and these false ideals often keep out the truth for ever.

The child should not be conscious of the restraint of external control through the personality of the teacher. The assertion of the personal will of the teacher inevitably leads to conflict and conscious resistance on the part of the child. This is the root of great evil. Through unconscious responsiveness the child should grow to conscious recognition of authority and obedience to law; and up to the highest condition of will culture, perfect self-control, and self-direction. The Divine will guides our wills in many ways that we do not understand or even recognise. Our control of childhood should be like Divine control in this respect.

External control that reveals its personality inevitably weakens the child's self-control, as external aid given unwisely necessarily destroys its self-reliance. Most children are injured by being helped too much. The child whose foolishly fond mother rushes to pick it up when it falls is usually hurt more by the picking up than by the fall; so the child who looks to parent or teacher as its only controlling agency will never fully develop its own self-control. Self-control develops in the same way as all other powers of self-expression or self-direction—by regular and progressive exercise. The child should be led to feel its individual responsibility, for a child's duty not a man's, as early as possible, and allowed to direct its own powers toward the accomplishment of its own purposes, limited by the law defining the rights of others. Reverence for the majesty of the law is a mightier force in character-building than yielding to the will of a teacher. Submission to law is an element of true manhood; meré subserviency to a human being is a characteristic of a slave. The child who is forced to submit passively and continuously to the personal domination of its teacher can never have true conceptions of liberty and individual responsibility.

It is utterly degrading to give pupils the idea that they are naturally expected to do wrong and that the teacher's constant duty is to check their natural tendencies. We should have faith in children. They deserve our faith, and if they do not, we may make them worthy of faith by trusting them. Let a boy understand that you expect him to do wrong, and he will usually fulfil your expectations. Boys love the right better than the wrong. They prefer the true to the false. They like to do good (not to be lectured about doing good) better than to do evil. They would rather produce than destroy. They love activity because it gives life; they hate passivity because it leads to death. Even if a boy is bad, inspiration is a grander controlling force than coercion. The most complete belief in the depravity of a child's nature does not justify the destruction of its spontaneity. Natural tendency may not always be toward the divine; natural power is always divine, and may become the controlling agency in correcting wrong tendency. Bad tempers and evil dispositions are defined in the consciousness of a child by criticism and coercion. Such defining is necessarily evil. The wise teacher is never saddened by the exhibition of strength and force by a child, even if they are manifested in selfish forms. The child with most power for evil should become strongest for good with wise training. The teacher's skill is shown by transforming power, not by destroying it. Teachers should remember that when the child comes to school it is in an advanced stage of its training. Human agencies by improper control or by equally improper freedom, or usually by a dreadful mixture of both, have been destroying the true spontaneity of the child.

All control is wrong that attempts to fetter the child with a man's thoughts, a man's motives, or a man's creed. Herein lies the greatest danger. It is a fatal blunder to rob a child of its childhood. We interfere too often with a child's spontaneity by checking its plays or by rousing it from its reveries. Teachers should remember that what would be folly or indolence in them may be absolutely essential for the highest development of the child physically, intellectually, and morally. A child may be injured morally by stopping its play with the sand on the seashore, or its ramble among the flowers, or its apparently idle dream as it lies looking at the clouds, to force it to listen to religious exercises it does not understand. The music of the birds and bees is more likely to arouse its spiritual nature than the music of an organ. He is the best teacher who most clearly remembers the feelings and thoughts of his own boyhood. We can not force maturity on a child in feeling, motive, thought, or action without making it a hypocrite, and we can make nothing worse out of it. The darkest hour in a child's life is the hour when it draws a curtain over the windows of its heart to shut out mother or teacher, and deceit usurps the place of honest frankness. It is easy for a child to degenerate when those in authority over it make it a hypocrite, and turn the life-producing waters of its free, responsive nature into a stagnant pool. Evil habits are poisonous growths springing from the trunks of decaying powers, and nourished by the sap intended to develop holy inspirations.

The motives of men and women are not those that stir children's lives to activity. The child rises from high to higher motives if properly guided.

Growth can not be forced, and the attempt to force it checks spontaneity and weakens individuality. Teachers often try to be power for their children, instead of guiding the powers already existing in the pupils. They try to force growth, or to restrict growth instead of providing the best conditions of growth, and reverently allowing growth to proceed in accordance with Divine law. They try to improve the flower queen by opening the rosebud instead of strengthening the rosebush. How grandly Nature's laws act! The sun never commands the flower to grow, nor does the rain say chidingly, "Drink or you shall not grow." The rain falls gently, the sun shines brightly, and the flowers become strong and beautiful.

Between opposites, Froebel always sought to find the mediation. Between control and spontaneity he discovered the mediation to be productive self-activity. Children love to work with material in harmony with their stage of development. Froebel used this love of work to develop the creative instinct, and at the same time to have the work done in accordance with limitations, or rules, or laws. He saw by careful study of childhood that children must have outlets for their energy, and he provided play and work to give them this outlet. He recognised the universal fact that "evil springs from unused good." Unused good becomes misused good, and produces evil. The same power that is intended to make the child constructive makes it destructive if wrongly used. The same tendency that undirected makes the anarchist will make a law-respecting citizen if guided wisely.

In the planning of the work to be done in the kindergarten, Froebel never forgot to lay down limitations within which, and rules by which, the child should do its work. These limitations and rules, however, did not interfere with the child's spontaneity. Within the limits and under the rules there was wide scope for variation, and each child was free to represent its own ideals as soon as, by working under the direction of the teacher, it had grasped the process of using the material supplied to it. The limitations and rules instead of interfering with its spontaneity, defined it, made it easier to exercise it consciously, and directed it into productive and therefore joy-giving channels.

The child, by its use of every gift and occupation of Froebel's system, is made a free agent, but it is free with the restriction of necessary law—law to which the kindergartner herself submits. In perforating, sewing, and drawing what Froebel called the "forms of beauty" or design, the child is restricted by the network lines used as the basis of the designs and by the law of symmetry. In most of the work done in these departments there is the additional restriction to lines limited in number, length, and direction. Definite law and logical order are followed even in the additions made from day to day in the number of lines and the variations allowed in their length and direction.

In mat-weaving, the pupils, even when they make their own designs, have to follow a regular plan, or combination of plans, in regard to the number of strips over and under the strip they are weaving in. Method, law, order, sequence are followed in all the steps made from the simplest "one up, one down," to the most complex combinations.

In colour-work, whether in mat-weaving or brush-work, the child is limited in the number of colours to be used.

In paper-folding there is a definite order to be followed in getting the foundation forms, and a regular sequence of transition from one form to another.

In paper-cutting there is a logical sequence for the preparatory folding and creasing of the paper, and for the cutting also; and the pasting of the resulting corresponding forms must be done in accordance with the law of symmetrical arrangement about a centre.

In making designs or objective forms, houses, bridges, tunnels, towers, stoves, sofas, etc., with the gifts, more than one law must be followed. The whole of the material must be used, and the various objects and buildings must be evolved. One structure must not be destroyed that another may be constructed from the ruins; the new one must be made by making a change from *the one already made.*

The law of unity, continuity, and harmony of opposites must be kept in mind in all the work of the child, so that it comes to recognise freedom within rule, liberty under law as a foundation principle, as something natural and necessary which becomes a part of its code of essential guiding principles.

In Froebel's plays the same submission to controlling laws is a part of the child's experience. Each child in playing is a free agent within the limits assigned to it and under the governing rules of the game. It performs its duty in the game as an independent individual, but is compelled to respect the rights of the other individuals composing the society to which it belongs. It could have no better training as an active member of society when it reaches maturity. In both its work and its play it finds itself under the reign of law which is beneficent and not cramping. Throughout Froebel's whole system he maintained the same perfect unity between control and spontaneity, and thus made the "perfect law of liberty" a part of the personal character of each child. When self-activity is carried out with a complete recognition of the supremacy of law, it becomes the surest basis for a conscious love of liberty.

He revealed the universality of law to the child by showing it that every plant grows in harmony with an inner law. Each variety of tree, shrub, and flower has its own method of branching, its own peculiar type of root, trunk or stalk, leaf and flower. Each member of any species is governed by the same law of growth. External conditions may modify the shape of the plant, but whether it grows to harmonious proportions in unimpeded freedom or is dwarfed and deformed by obstacles that interfere with its growth, it possesses the characteristic peculiarities of its class; it is stamped by the dominant law of its species.

By making self-activity within law the fundamental process in his system Froebel secured the perfect harmony between spontaneity and control. Selfhood and law are constantly respected in his system. They are never put at variance. The child is always self-directing, although at first it is guided in its self-direction. Self-effacement is never made the basis of self-control. From the first the child's will is active, because activity is the source of growth. The theory of stage development applies to the will as fully as to any other power. The will in the first stage should not be allowed to do the work it is expected to do in the higher stages of the evolution of its complete control. It may be guided and even aided, but it must be self-active if it is to grow to conscious power.

Anarchy is not the fierce son of freedom, but the cruel son of coercion. True freedom leaves the child no need for anarchy in Froebel's system, because it is joyously occupied at productive work. Mere freedom is not Froebel's mediation between control and spontaneity. He calls into complete development two dominating principles in the life of a well-balanced child—love of freedom and productive activity. The union of these forms the complete bond between the apparent opposites, and makes an organic unity of diverse elements, which is the most perfect type of unity according to Froebel.

Productive activity is the chief source of joy to childhood, and should be man's greatest fountain of pleasure if his training has given proper development to his natural tendency. There is no room for anarchy in the experience of a child or a man whose life is filled with opportunities for self-expression in any form of productive activity. Anarchy results chiefly from the overflow of repressed energy, which demands relief from coercion and finds relief in unnatural outlets. It is another illustration of the truth of Ruskin's aphorism, "All evil springs from unused (misused) good." The right use of the elements of character that make the anarchist would make of the same man a good member of society. Froebel would never let law and selfhood become divorced. His entire system aims to keep them in harmony, and to unfold this harmony more and more clearly till it becomes a controlling element in character.

One of the greatest powers the parent or teacher can exercise in the direction of children is the power to change the centre of interest from evil to good. Froebel refused to believe that children love to do wrong better than to do right. He believed that their dominant desire was to do. Whether to do right or wrong at first depends on environment and experience; afterward on habit and judgment. He knew that, even though they may become happier in doing right than in doing wrong, little children are not wise enough to decide what is right and what is wrong, and that they prefer to do—rather than not to do—even if they have to do wrong. He separated the doing from the thing done, and in this he was wiser than other educational philosophers. He said to teachers in effect: The child loves doing—*activity.* It loves better doing work that is the expression of its selfhood—*self-activity.* It loves best of all doing work that is the expression of its selfhood, and at the same time produces something of use—*productive self-activity.* Our duty as teachers is to guide the child so that its natural tendency to do may develop in manhood into the habit of productive self-activity. This will make the race most happy when engaged in productive work; not alone with material things, but in the higher realms of intellectual and spiritual work. Therefore he deplored most of all the fatal blunder that has been the leading characteristic of all discipline, both in the home and the school, of checking activity, because it was directed to wrong ends.

Activity results from a divinely implanted tendency which the Creator meant to be used energetically through life, and which is the motive power that impels man to labour in the conquest of Nature and in achieving the higher victories over evil. Triumph is the reward of conscious struggle. The power to struggle persistently lies at the foundation of grand character. Truly great characters are those who struggle most earnestly and most selfishly for the achievement of right. Childhood loves to encounter difficulties in play or in work. It is a natural instinct that leads it to exercise its powers to qualify it for a life work of overcoming. The teacher who checks activity in a child does a grievous wrong. The activity is right, even though its aim be wrong. Interest should lead to activity. It opposes the natural evolution of a child's powers in the most positive and the most pernicious way to permit its interest to be aroused so thoroughly as to lead it to definite activity, and then dogmatically and coercively check the activity and block the way to the accomplishment of its purpose. Nothing can contribute more to the destruction of character power, and the substitution of inertness for activity and negativeness for positiveness, than the persistent stopping of activity. It weakens interest and the tendency to achievement, and thus robs the child of both the motive and the power to act.

"Stop," "Don't," and "Be quiet," have been the leading words in a teacher's vocabulary of discipline. Before Froebel revolutionized discipline commands were enforced by terrorism. The teacher was a tyrant and the pupil a slave. Authority was founded on force, and respect for it on fear. These were the conditions best calculated to develop selfishness, hatred of law, disrespect for authority, and therefore to foster the spirit of anarchy.

But the chief evil of the system of repression is the destruction of force of character. The lessening of the child's interest in life, and the weakening of its tendency to execute its plans and decisions. The very powers on which intellectual development and storing and executive achievement depend most, and which the teacher should aim most to cultivate, are those which were checked continually before Froebel's time.

Froebel's separation of the love of doing from the end of the doing enabled him to solve the greatest problem in discipline by the substitution of a change in the interest centre in place of the old and still too common practice of stopping the child's activity. The power to change the centre of interest from wrong to right constitutes the highest disciplinary ability a teacher can possess. The skilful teacher never requires to say "Stop" or "Don't." The world is so full of wonders and of beautiful, attractive things that the teacher should always be able to turn the interested attention from wrong to right, or to revive exhausted interest and listless attention by changing the centre of interest. It may require close study of children's interests to do this effectively, but no study will pay better. To destroy the child's interest saps its intellectual life and energy. This is a crime against the individual and the race. It is little better to distract attention by temporary expedients or by greater energy and enthusiasm on the part of the teacher. This still leaves the child in a negative condition, because it makes attention the end of the process. Attention that ends in attention can not be long sustained. Unless it leads to independent, progressive, intellectual activity, interest soon dies, and the child is left in an inert mental condition. The teacher can not long remain the centre of interest to the child. No adult should assume to control the interest of even a single child. It is impossible to sustain real interest in a class by talking, by exhibiting pictures or objects, or even by performing experiments. To listen, to look, or to observe leaves the child in a receptive condition. Sustained interest demands more than this. True character growth intellectually and spiritually calls for more than this. Interest must lead to activity in some form on the part of the child itself. Even when changing the centre of the child's interest the teacher should lead to the new interest without making the child conscious of interference. The tactful teacher usually gets the suggestion of new interest centres from the pupils.

Productive self-activity sustains interest and prevents the inattention and the mischief-making so common in the schools of former times. There should be no occasion for the scolding and checking still too often practised. Many teachers still check the natural tendency to activity till their pupils become idle, and then scold them for being idle. When the harmony between control and spontaneity is thoroughly understood and based on the child's productive self-activity, there will be no need for what has been called discipline in the schools. "There is no need of any constraint or any command for that activity which is in harmony with the being of man in general, and at the same time with his individual disposition. It will act freely with love, and not overstep the measure of the powers at different ages." Activity under law produces harmony and development; inertness under law leads to anarchy and deterioration.

Spontaneity in productive self-activity develops active instead of passive obedience, co-operation instead of obstinacy and stubbornness, activity instead of inertia of character, energy instead of indolence, positiveness instead of negativeness, cheerfulness instead of dulness, and independence instead of subserviency.

The extensive recognition of the universality of the principle of human liberty demands that all children be trained under such conditions as will develop a conscious recognition of the perfect harmony between law and liberty. Such an education Froebel planned to give. During its stage of unconscious imitation the child should be directed within the limitations of necessary rules and principles in the accomplishment of its own purposes. The direction of the superior mind does not weaken the child's selfhood unless the teacher makes the child conscious of the direction. When it becomes "personal or arbitrary," direction becomes destructive. Direction followed without consciousness of subordination should gradually lead to conscious recognition of law, and responsibility, and individual power and freedom. This is the true ideal of unity between control and spontaneity. It is impossible to give a young man a clear comprehension of this unity, and its full meaning in developing self-government, self-restraint, self-direction, and self-reliance, coupled with a definite conception of the relationship between individual and universal human rights, and of law as the most complete expression of these rights, by a theoretical exposition of its principles. Courses in colleges and universities on social science and political economy can never truly become vital elements in a man's character unless he has apperceptive centres of experience to correspond to them.

Froebel, by his fundamental principle of discipline or child guidance, has in two generations revolutionized the schools. They are no longer places for the exercise of tyrannical coercion and passive obedience. Kindness has taken the place of severity, and sadness has been driven out by the sunlight of joyousness. The twentieth century will make schools what Froebel wished them to be—"Free republics of childhood." How much that phrase means!

The truest educational progress of the ages has been toward harmony between control and spontaneity, guidance and freedom, obedience and independence, submission and liberty. Freedom is the only basis broad enough on which to rest a system of education. We should aim to secure free growth; not the wild growth of the jungle, but the free, assisted growth of the best cultivated garden. "No man is free who is not master of himself," said Epictetus. It is self-evident that no man can be master of himself who is not free. Only through freedom can he fully know the self he has to master.

The Baroness von Marenholtz-Bülow wisely says: "Childhood's unconscious lesson to us is that what is undeveloped can without guidance never be free, but, left to itself, must inevitably fall into caprice. Guidance capacitates for freedom. It is a dominant error of our age to demand freedom where the capacity for freedom is still lacking." This truth may lead to error unless the corresponding truth that freedom means nothing to undeveloped selfhood is as clearly recognised. We should prepare our pupils for fruit-bearing at maturity, but we should never try to make them "bear to pattern," as Dr. Blimber did. The child should be controlled, but control should consist in letting the sunshine into its life, that it may be stirred to action, and through action grow to greater life.

The proper use of power in all stages of a man's development is the most certain way of revealing true freedom and preventing its misuse. Froebel condensed this central educational thought into two short sentences: "The will is strengthened *only by voluntary* activity. By striving to create the beautiful and the good, the feelings are developed, and by all *lawful, thoughtful, free* activity the mind is cultivated."

By lawful, thoughtful, free, productive self-activity from childhood to maturity man is prepared for the struggle of each soul "to break its fetters and lead to freedom—that is, to that freedom which recognises law as its first principle, and submits to it *consciously*."

Froebel's work has influenced the work of discipline more than any other department of school work, but the improvement has resulted chiefly from the objective lessons in loving kindness and sympathy given in the kindergarten. The underlying philosophy of the law of harmony between control and spontaneity is not yet fully understood by teachers. When it is clearly comprehended universally, all schools will become "Free republics of childhood."

CHAPTER VII.

NATURE AS THE REVEALER OF LIFE, EVOLUTION, AND GOD.

SOME educators yet maintain that Nature study has no influence on moral education. Froebel made Nature the chief agency outside of the home in laying the foundation in the child's mind for the comprehension of religious truth, as through it he revealed to the child life, evolution, power to help other life to better life, and God himself. He says:

"Education as instruction should lead man to see and know the divine, spiritual, and eternal principle which animates surrounding Nature, constitutes the essence of Nature, and is permanently manifested in Nature."

"Indeed, life in and with Nature, and with the fair, silent things of Nature, should be fostered at this time by parents and other members of the family as *a chief fulcrum of child life.*"

"The Spirit of God rests in Nature, lives and reigns in Nature, is expressed in Nature, is communicated by Nature, is developed and cultivated in Nature—yet Nature is not the body of God."

"As we study the works of man, how much more

then should we endeavour to know *Nature,* the work of God, to acquaint ourselves with the objects of Nature in their life, their significance, in their relation to the Spirit of God."

"Nature and man have their origin in one and the same eternal Being, and their development takes place in accordance with the same laws, only at different stages."

"The observation of Nature and the observation of man are mutually explanatory, and naturally lead to deeper knowledge, the one of the other."

"Man—particularly in boyhood—should become intimate with Nature, not so much with reference to the details and outer forms of her phenomena, as with reference to the Spirit of God that lives in her and rules over her. Indeed, the boy feels this deeply, and demands it; for this reason, where love of Nature is still unimpaired, nothing perhaps unites teachers and pupils so intimately as the thoughtful study of Nature."

"The boy—the learning human being—should at an early period be taught to see Nature in all her diversity *as a unit,* as a great living whole, as one thought of God. The integrity of Nature as a continuously developing whole must be shown him at an early period. Without a knowledge of this unity in the activities and forms of Nature, it is impossible to attain or to impart a genuine knowledge of natural history."

"The things of Nature form a more beautiful ladder between heaven and earth than that seen by Jacob; not a one-sided ladder leading in one direction, but an all-sided one leading in all directions."

"All that is told in Genesis of the history of creation

is lived by the child in his kindergarten education. Instead of words he needs his own experience; his garden work teaches him that the growth of plants does not depend upon himself or upon human power, but that an invisible power governs it. This teaches him almost without words to find the Creator."

"I can still see my hazel buds, like angels, opening for me the great God's temple of Nature."

"I have ever thankfully enjoyed what Nature has spread before my eyes, and she has always been in true motherly unity with me."

"Living cheerfully and joyfully in the bosom of Nature with my first pupils, I began to tell myself that the training of natural life was closely akin to the training of human life."

"Man is compelled not only to recognise Nature in her manifold forms and appearances, but also to understand her in the unity of her inner working, of her effective force. Therefore he himself follows Nature's methods in the course of his own development and culture, and in his games he imitates Nature at her work of creation."

"Every contact with Nature elevates, strengthens, purifies."

"As I wandered on in the sunlit, far-stretching hills, or along the still shore of the lake, clear as crystal, smooth as a mirror, or in the shady groves, under the tall forest trees, my spirit grew full with ideas of the truly Godlike nature and priceless value of a man's soul, and I gladdened myself with the consideration of mankind as the beloved children of God."

"When I was consulted by others, I looked to Nature for the answer, and let Nature, life, spirit, and law speak for themselves through me."

These quotations from Froebel's writings prove that he was one of the prophet souls of Nature. The symbolism of Nature as a revealer of life, unity, development, human evolution, and God, illuminated Froebel's mind and made him a true poet. Though he wrote not in the rhythmic metre of the poets, the rhythmic melody filled his life, and made him the poetical philosopher of Nature as Wordsworth was her philosophical poet. Mr. Bowen has shown how much alike Froebel and Wordsworth were in their love for Nature and their interpretation of her symbolism. These two were Nature's deepest philosophers. They reached the great Nature heart about the same time (Froebel a little earlier) and independently. To Froebel may be given the honour of seeing first "that the training of natural life is closely akin to the training of human life," and of working this thought out practically as a part of his educational system. Of the writers before Froebel, Pope had the clearest conception of the unity between Nature, man, and God. In his Essay on Man he says:

> All are but parts of one stupendous whole,
> Whose body Nature is, and God the soul."

Wordsworth expressed the same thought over and over again:

> Happy is he who lives to understand
> Not human nature only, but explores
> All natures, to the end that he may find
> The law that governs each; and where begins
> The union, the partition where, that makes
> Kind and degree among all visible beings;

The constitutions, powers, and faculties,
Which they inherit—can not step beyond—
And can not fall beneath; that do assign
To every class its station and its office,
Through all the mighty commonwealth of things,
Up from the creeping plant to sovereign man.

To every form of being is assigned
An *active* principle; howe'er removed
From sense and observation, it subsists
In all things, in all natures, in the stars
Of azure heaven, the unenduring clouds,
In flower and tree, in every pebbly stone
That paves the brooks, the stationary rocks,
The moving waters, and the invisible air.

Since the time of Froebel and Wordsworth many great thinkers have learned the symbolism of Nature, and have woven it into song or story. The fact that these advanced leaders of a developing race have had their minds filled with this vital thought indicates that the race itself is nearing the stage in its evolution when it will comprehend the thought and make it an impelling force in its upward progress.

Longfellow, in writing of flowers, says:

In all places then, and in all seasons,
  Flowers expand their light and soul-like wings;
Teaching us by most persuasive reasons,
  How akin they are to human things.

And with childlike, credulous affection
  We behold their tender buds expand,
Emblems of our own great resurrection:
  Emblems of the bright and better land.

Tennyson beautifully expresses the same thought:

> Flower in the crannied wall,
> I pluck you out of your crannies,
> Hold you here, root and all, in my hand,
> Little flower—but if I could understand
> What you are, root and all, and all in all,
> I should know what God and man is.

To Froebel the active principle in Nature was God. He saw this active principle in all things—the stars, the sky, the clouds, the flowers, the trees, the brooks, and even in the rocks. He believed that to every child Nature speaks clearly and tenderly of this life. Even though the child may not be conscious of the fact, its life is enriched by an intimate acquaintance with Nature as it can be in no other way. Nature was to Froebel a stimulating atmosphere in which the whole intellectual and spiritual being is invigorated, and through which God makes to the child manifold revelations. Therefore he said to parents: "Take your little children by the hand; go with them into Nature as into the house of God. Allow the wee one to stroke the good cow's forehead, and run about among the fowl, and play at the edge of the wood. Make companions for your boys and girls of the trees and the banks and the pasture land." He meant a great deal by companionship with Nature. The living principle in Nature was so real to him as to give personality even to inanimate things. Nature was not the body of God to him, but God was the living principle in all things. He did not expect the child to become conscious of God at first, but he did wish it to recognise life in all the growing things around it, in order that it might when older know God as the source of life, and as the universal life essence. Loving companionship with the life of Nature in unconscious childhood becomes loving unity with God in the conscious life of maturity.

Froebel would have the child live amid the life of Nature for many reasons. He did not believe it possible to develop the religious nature of man fully if childhood has not received through association with Nature conceptions of life, of life stimulation, and of invisible life behind life, as the source of life and the guide of life. Such experience qualifies for the recognition of spiritual life and of a spiritual Creator. The reawakening of the trees and flowers in spring, and the development of a butterfly from the worm through the chrysalis stage, make it possible to conceive the idea of man's resurrection, and by analogy reveal death as a joyous transition into a broader, freer life, and not as the end of life. Even the thought of the love of the Creator grows gradually in the mind of a child who sees the loving attention of the mother birds, and recognises through this the loving kindness of its own mother. There is a natural progressive sequence in the recognition of the love of bird or domestic animal, of mother and of God. The highest ideal in relation to any subject is never possible unless the groundwork for the mature ideal is laid in corresponding experiences of a kind adapted to the ages preceding maturity. This is especially true of abstract ideals. They can not find a sure resting place in the mind unless there are already in the mind symbolic representations corresponding to them. Nature is a wondrous field for constructive symbolism. The purest men and women are those who retain through life their responsive susceptibility to the symbolic teaching and companionship of Nature.

Froebel hoped to reveal progressive evolution to higher life to the child through Nature. Beginning with the least developed forms of vegetable life, Nature presents a continuous, ascending series of steps, each step revealing wider, freer life as we rise through the vegetable kingdom and animal life to man himself. It is perfectly natural to carry on this progressive evolution at the proper time beyond man and up to God, the invisible spiritual life, that has manifested itself through the unity and the life of Nature.

He urged very strongly that all children should be trained to cultivate plants, partly in order to gratify their natural tendency to work in the earth, and to use their interest in productive activity and the nurture of living things, especially plants or pets. But he had higher reasons for making every child a little gardener, both at home and at school. Careful culture in the preparation of the soil and its proper enrichment, coupled with due attention to watering, weeding, hoeing, and, if necessary, to pruning, produces plants of grander proportions, greater beauty, and richer fruitfulness. By these results the child not only learns to recognise evolution, but it also sees that it may become an active agent in promoting evolution. It gains a conception—at first symbolic, afterward conscious—of the greatest of all truths—*that it has power to help other life to grow to grander life.* By sowing the apparently dead seed, which afterward bursts into life and beauty, it learns that it has power to start life to grow that without its aid might have remained for ever undeveloped. The teacher or parent does not require to point the lesson. The symbolism of the unconscious stage of childhood will naturally become transformed into conscious character in due time. It is impossible to overestimate the advantages of a training that, through the self-activity of a child, reveals to it the two vital truths—that it may aid all life—human life as well as plant life—to reach a higher condition of life, and that it may bring into existence new elements of living power, material power, intellectual power, or spiritual power, to aid in unifying and uplifting the race. The formation of these apperceptive centres in a child's mind qualifies it for the highest education it can ever receive. The life must remain comparatively barren in which these ideals have not been implanted. The time to implant them is the symbolic period of childhood, and the process is the nurture of life in Nature. The phenomena of Nature in their everyday manifestations provide most appropriate symbolism for children. They are thrice blessed whose early life is stimulated and enriched by free life in sympathy with Nature's life.

Froebel's fundamental law, as we have seen, is unity, inner connection, or interrelatedness. The perfect revelation of this law as the basis of the social organization of the race by the union of consciously responsible individuals he made the chief work of college and university training. The symbolic foundation, or apperceptive centres for such a perfect revelation, he claimed must be gained in childhood and partly from Nature. He regarded a tree as the most perfect material symbol of unity.

The objects and processes of Nature are, in Froebel's opinion, the best agencies for the development of the imagination. They supply the greatest variety of elements for the imagination to use, and they stimulate the child's creative faculty in many lines of work, laying the foundation for constructive imagery in maturity in artistic, scientific, mathematical, literary, and ethical work. The elements of life and progressive evolution in Nature have an influence on the imagination, and suggest to the mind the constructive readjustment of its store of knowledge. Nature is nowhere a mere storehouse of elements. She transforms inorganic matter into organized life, and the mind is roused to similar organic work by familiarity with Nature's processes.

The beauty, the symmetry, the harmony, the life, the freedom, the purity, the majesty, and the invisible forces of Nature fill the mind with images that elevate and ennoble character. When these pure images are photographed on the sensitive nature of childhood, they can never be eradicated. When the pictures are developed by whatever experiences or circumstances, they are still pure, and help to counterbalance the evil that may come into our lives. What better thing can the parents and teachers of a child do for it than to train it so that, as Wordsworth said, it may become in maturity—

> One whose heart the holy forms
> Of young imagination have kept pure.

Wordsworth expressed in many exquisite lines the purifying and strengthening influence of Nature on the imagination. The Excursion teems with rapturous references such as these:

> . . . Nature fails not to provide
> Impulse and utterance. The whispering air
> Sends inspiration from the shadowy heights
> And blind recesses of the caverned rocks;

> While, free as air, o'er printless sands we march,
> And pierce the gloom of her majestic woods,
> Roaming or resting under grateful shade,
> In peace and meditative cheerfulness;
> Where living things, and things inanimate,
> Do speak, at Heaven's command, to eye and ear,
> And speak to social reason's inner sense,
> With inarticulate language.
>
> . . . For the man
> Who, in this spirit, communes with the forms
> Of Nature; who, with understanding heart,
> Doth know and love such objects as excite
> No morbid passions, no disquietude,
> No vengeance, and no hatred, needs must feel
> So deeply, that, unsatisfied with aught
> Less pure and exquisite, he can not choose
> But seek for objects of a kindred love
> In fellow natures and a kindred joy.

The child's first questionings are about Nature if it lives close to her. The spirit of investigation, the wonder spirit, the power of problem discovery, is aroused and developed more fully by her myriad mysteries than in any other way. She has unsolved questions adapted to early childhood, and continues to reveal new phenomena to match man's unfolding powers.

There is a never-failing field of intense interest to a child in friendly association and intimate acquaintance with birds, butterflies, bees, beetles, ants, and worms. The child attaches a personality to each of them, and will spend hours in watching them at their work. It needs little tact on the part of mother or teacher to make their interest reverent instead of destructive, as it too often is. Mother's example is better than her precepts. A wise mother will promise the little one a visit to-morrow to new friends, and, when the child has been prepared for a visit as carefully as if going to visit at a friend's house, will take it by the hand and lead it perhaps to an ant's nest, and, seating herself with her child where they will not disturb the ants, will say, "Good morning, little ants; we have come to see you at work." The child will be more interested in such a visit than in going to a neighbour's house. Mothers, too, may learn many interesting things from their insect neighbours.

After a few such visits, the child may be trusted to go alone among its flying or creeping friends, and it will often spend several hours each day in loving companionship with them, sometimes talking to them as if they were able to understand all it said. Who can tell what symbolic representations of life and work are taken into the child's unconscious life during these visits? How the imagination grows as each nest is filled with imaginary characters! What tales are told to the child even by the worms! That ant performing its allotted task preaches a sermon to the child better for it than the formal theology of the minister. What songs of joy and merriment the birds and crickets sing! How contentedly the bees hum at their work! These stories and sermons and songs weave themselves into the fibre of the child's nature, and give sweetness and vigour and charm to its whole life. The simple fact that by such association the child is trained to love birds, animals, and insects, and to be kind to them instead of cruel, makes a marked difference in its character.

Froebel urged parents and teachers to take their

children and pupils regularly for walks into the country and, if possible, into the heart of Nature in the woods, and by the speaking waters of stream, or lake, or sea. "It is so important," he says, "that boys and adults should go into the fields and forests together striving to receive into their hearts and minds the life and spirit of Nature, which would soon put an end to the idle, useless, and indolent loafing of so many boys."

In all such excursions, and in all the child's experience with Nature, he taught that the life in Nature should be reverenced. He would not allow animals or insects to be tortured, or plant life to be recklessly destroyed, for the gratification of misguided interest or of a passionate love for flower beauty. He aimed to make love of flower life develop into a desire to help flower life to better, stronger, higher life by attention and culture, as a revelation of power to aid all life, instead of leading to selfishness and sensuality by allowing the child to destroy the life of the flower to satisfy his passionate love for it. Love that becomes mere desire for possession is always debasing. The greater the power of any element of character to elevate, the greater its power to degrade if misused.

If children are allowed to pull the wild flowers in the woods without restraint, they will do so to gratify the desire for possession of the thing that gives them pleasure. Persistence in such a course must lead to evil. The children will become careless about the destruction of life, and reverence for life is a most important part of a child's training. They will learn to believe that desire should always lead to possession—a most immoral principle that all training should counteract. Liberty to the child in the gratification of desire for beautiful things leads to libertinism in the gratification of desire for beautiful things in manhood. Flower love is a sacred feeling, but when it degenerates in childhood into mere selfish desire for possession, as it is nearly always allowed to do, it becomes a sure germ for sensuality in manhood. Sensuality is but the debasement of sacred feelings. The boy who is allowed to destroy flower life to satisfy desire is being trained to sacrifice other life and beauty for his selfish gratification in manhood. Self-restraint is one of the most essential moral forces; self-indulgence, even in pure and beautiful things, is always destructive of character. This is especially true when life of any kind is saved by the self-restraint or sacrificed by the self-indulgence.

Froebel made it a special aim to lead children to admire beautiful things without developing a desire for their possession. In his light songs the foundation for this important character development is laid. In dealing with flowers and other beautiful things in Nature the same principle is carefully followed. What a change would be effected in the character of the race if Froebel's principle were universally carried out in the training of childhood!

Reverence for life developed through the nurture of life should receive careful attention in all primary schools. Children should sow seeds in boxes in the school windows and in beds in the schoolyards, and the children themselves should be trained to supply the needs of the flowers. The plants grown by the children will form the most interesting basis for observation lessons, and for language and reading lessons; but by far the most important lesson to be learned from the flowers is reverence for life, and a consciousness that each child has power to help other life to better life.

The study of Nature has greatly enriched school courses in material for thought, and has also led to an improvement and extension in the form studies. Making, modelling, and painting are finding a place in schools as means of expression largely through the attention paid to Nature study.

Throughout England many societies have recently been organized to protect flowers, and to extend the love of flowers by sowing seeds and planting bulbs and roots in waste places. Another aim of the societies is to awaken an interest in window gardening in the homes of working people. These societies are called "Mary's Meadow Societies," and they are named after Mrs. Evans's charming little book, entitled Mary's Meadow. Every school in the world should be a "Mary's Meadow Society." The training in love of flowers, in reverence for flower life, in flower nurture, and in desire to add to the happiness of others by increased attention to flower culture would be a most important element in moral training. Schools in different continents or widely separated parts of continents might exchange wild-flower seeds, and thus the range of beautiful wild-flower growth might be greatly extended.

In his letter to the Duke of Meiningen, Froebel wrote very strongly about the advantages of the study of Nature. After describing his joyous experiences in the classes, and especially in the museum in Berlin, where he found that "what he had recognised in things great or noble, or in the life of man, or in the ways of God, as serving toward the development of the human race, he could recognise also in the smallest of these fixed forms which Nature alone had shaped," he goes on to say, " Nature and man now seem to me mutually to explain each other, through all their numberless, various stages of development; " and concludes by saying that he became " penetrated and absorbed by the thought " that the " foundation for and the guidance toward a knowledge of himself and of life, and a preparation for the manifestation of that knowledge " which man receives through sympathetic love and study of Nature, " is beyond all else vital to man's culture and development, to the sure attainment of his destiny and fulfilment of his vocation."

Froebel pleaded in a hundred ways for the " tender fostering of the primitive and natural inclinations of every human being in the germ " in childhood. Unless they are so fostered he has no hope of perfect development in manhood. In his own life, he says gratefully, they were satisfied by " the influence of Nature, of useful handiwork and religious feelings." His friend Diesterweg recommends a similar course of early training for childhood. Speaking of his own training, he says: " From my youth I loved the woods and mountains. We boys spent more time in the mountains, the woods, and the founderies than we did in the schools." Wordsworth describes himself as one—

> . . . Whose favourite school
> Hath been the fields, the roads, and rural lanes.

All three make Nature the best friend of childhood, the atmosphere which nourishes the germs of pure and noble character.

Wordsworth, the philosophic poet of Nature, so appropriately complements Froebel, the poet-philosopher of Nature, it seems fitting to allow him to be the final interpreter of Froebel's views in regard to the subject they both understood so well:

. . . Nature never did betray
The heart that loved her.

Come forth into the light of things,
Let Nature be your teacher.

Sweet is the lore which Nature brings.

To me the meanest flower that blows can give
Thoughts that do often lie too deep for tears.

. . . What good is given to men,
More solid than the gilded clouds of heaven,
What joy more lasting than a vernal flower.

. . . For I have learned
To look on Nature, not as in the hour
Of thoughtless youth.
. . . .

And I have felt
A presence that disturbs me with the joy
Of elevated thoughts; a sense sublime
Of something far more deeply interfused,
Whose dwelling is the light of setting suns,
And the round ocean, and the living air,
And the blue sky, and in the mind of man:
A motion and a spirit, that impels
All thinking things, all objects of all thought,
And rolls through all things. Therefore am I still
A lover of the meadows, and the woods,
And mountains; and of all that we behold
From this green earth; of all the mighty world

Of eye and ear, both what they half create,
And what perceive; well pleased to recognise
In Nature and the language of the sense
The anchor of my purest thoughts, the nurse,
The guide, the guardian of my heart, and soul
Of all my moral being.

CHAPTER VIII.

CORRELATION OF STUDIES.

CORRELATION is defined as "mutual or reciprocal relation, or the act of bringing under relations of union correspondence or interaction." *

Froebel regarded unity or inner connection as the most important law in education, and comprehended it more fully than any other educator. He did not write so much about correlation as Herbart under the title correlation, but he made it a foundation law of his system, not alone in regard to studies, as we have seen in Chapter III, but in regard to the stages of man's development; the training of his physical, intellectual, and spiritual nature; the culture of his receptive, reflective, and executive powers; the relationship of Nature, man, and God, and of the individual and the race; and the harmonizing of apparent opposites. He wrought unity into every part of his system so far as he completed it. The kindergarten is still the most perfect educational type of correlation. In every good kindergarten there is a clearly defined central purpose in the work of every day to which every song, story, occupation, and game is re-

* The Standard Dictionary.

lated. This is equally true of the work of each week or month. The work of the year should be an organic whole, and in the outline plan of the kindergartner the work of each month, and week, and day should be logically related to this whole. While sufficiently elastic to admit of infinite variety, and to take advantage of incidental occurrences and circumstances, the kindergartner's plan should be definite, and framed with a conscious purpose. There can be no haphazard work in the kindergarten if it is conducted in accordance with Froebel's principles. Each year should accomplish a certain part in the child's evolution, and each month, and week, and day should have its part in the natural evolution. It is admitted that the kindergarten is the best educational type of correlation, and, as an objective representation of correlation, it is helping to make the importance of the subject known and its principles clear. It is to be regretted that Froebel was unable to organize his system more fully above the kindergarten.

His most distinctive characteristic as an educator was his organization of every fundamental principle into educational methods. His ability in thus reducing theories to practice was so marked that Mr. Bowen says of him: "All the ideas which he used may in a sense be called his from the way in which he organized them and applied them to education."

While a boy at the school in Stadt-Ilm, where he went to live with his uncle when he was ten years of age, he noticed the utter lack of interrelation or connectedness between the studies. Writing of his experiences at that period, he says: "In physical geography we repeated our tasks parrotwise, *speaking much and knowing noth-*

ing; for the teaching on this subject had not the very least connection with real life, nor had it any actuality for us, although at the same time we could rightly name *our little specks and patches of colour on the map.* I received private tuition in this subject also. My teacher wished to advance further with me; he took me to England. I could find no connection between that country and the place and country in which I dwelt myself; so that of this instruction also I retained but little. As for actual instruction in German, it was not to be thought of; but we received directions in letter writing and spelling. I do not know with what study the teaching of spelling was connected, but I think it was not connected with any; *it hovered in the air.*"

While attending lectures in Berlin he maintained himself by teaching in a private school. Here, too, he noted the fact that there was a lack of "unity in the course of instruction. Everywhere I sought for recognition of the quickening interconnection of parts, and for the exposition of the inner all-pervading reign of law. Only a few lectures made some poor approach to such methods, but I found nothing of the sort in those which were most important to me, physics and mathematics. Especially repugnant to me was the *piecemeal patchwork* offered to us in geometry, always separating and dividing, never uniting and consolidating."

When, at the age of twenty-five, he was a teacher of three boys in a private family, his dominant ideal began to define itself more clearly. Writing of this period, he says: "What especially lay heavy upon me at this time was the utter absence of any organized connection between the subjects of education."

When twenty-six years of age he took his three lads with him to Yverdun, in order that he might study the system and methods of Pestalozzi. Again he was disappointed. He found inspiration and many new methods of teaching individual subjects, but the inner connection for which he longed above all else was wanting. "Each separate branch of education," he writes, "was in such a condition as to powerfully interest, but never wholly to content the observer, since it prepared only further division and separation and did not tend toward unity. The want of unity of effort, both as to means and aims, I soon felt; I recognised it in the inadequacy, the incompleteness, and the unlikeness of the ways in which the various subjects were taught." Summing up the results of his two years' study of Pestalozzi's work at Yverdun, he says: "On the whole, I passed a glorious time at Yverdun, elevated in tone, and critically decisive for my after life. At its close, however, I felt more clearly than ever the deficiency of inner unity and interdependence, as well as of outward comprehensiveness and thoroughness in the teaching there." So strongly was he impressed by this conception of the lack of a proper correlation of the subjects of education that he made the revealing of unity as the fundamental law of education the aim of his life. "I became impelled by an irresistible impulse toward the setting forth of unity and simplicity with all the force, both of my pen and of my life, in the shape of an educational system. I felt that education as well as science would gain by what I may call a more human, related, affiliated, connected treatment and consideration of the subjects of education."

To reveal *connectedness* became the great purpose of

his life. He did not confine connectedness to the subjects of instruction. He regarded it as the vital law of human development, and taught that the chief work of the colleges and universities lies in defining man's ideals of social unity and racial interrelationship. The Committee of Fifteen agree with this view. Their report says: "For higher education seems to have as its province the correlation of the several branches of human learning *in the unity* of the spiritual view furnished by religion to our civilization." Limiting the meaning of unity, connectedness, or correlation to the subjects of study, Froebel made Nature the connecting centre through which the child could be most easily and most completely led to study other subjects. He objected strongly to any formal, artificial, or mechanical affiliation between the subjects. Each study should be related to the central subject directly and logically as part of an essential process in its complete unfolding. Under the general term "Nature" he included mineralogy, geology, chemistry, crystallography, botany, zoölogy, biology, physics, and for the purposes of a central relating study he included objects constructed by man as well as the works of God.

He related language and grammar to Nature because "complete preparation for a *thorough knowledge of language* and thorough skill in its use implies three things: First, the observation of the sensuous objects of language—the observation of the outer world; secondly, the observation of language and objects in connection with one another, passing from the outer to the inner world—exercise in language; lastly, observation of language as such, without reference to the objects designated—grammatical exercises." As Nature presents concrete objects she gives the child clear conceptions, and clear thinking is the basis of exact language. As she presents such varied forms and conditions it requires an enlarging vocabulary to express the thoughts she arouses. As she reveals her fundamental laws and methods of growth she leads to classification of conceptions, and therefore to logical thought and expression. Language can be readily and profitably co-ordinated with Nature study. He found it very hard to study a foreign language, especially its grammar, in the fragmentary manner in which it is usually taught, and felt the need of connectedness in some way between his own personal life and purposes and the language he attempted to learn. In describing his efforts to learn Latin, he says: "It always seemed to me as if the mere outer acquisition of a language could but little help forward my true inner desire for knowledge, which was deeply in earnest and was the result of my own free choice. But wherever the knowledge of language linked itself to definite external impressions, and I was able to perceive its connection with facts—as, for instance, in the scientific nomenclature of botany—I could quickly make myself master of it." The development of the language power has been too artificial in the schools. Composition and oral expression have been divorced from the life of the child. The clear expression of the definite thought in the child's mind immediately associated with the subject under consideration has received little attention, and composition has been assigned at remote periods, the subjects usually being abstractions of a most uninteresting character. Little wonder that it has been one of the least profitable and most formal exercises of the school.

The leaders in educational work are beginning to learn that the accurate expression of the results of a pupil's own investigation in science or literature or mathematics or history in the regular work of the schoolroom, both orally and in written form, is the best way to develop the language power, and define the power of accurate thinking. Accurate thinking leads to accuracy of expression, and accuracy of expression defines accurate thinking. This idea of composition in connection with the regular work of the child is Froebel's idea of the true correlation of language with other subjects. He objected to have any of the language departments—reading, writing, spelling. composition, grammar, or literature—"hovering in the air." They should be sug- by the other subjects of study and should react upon them. As Nature in all its forms is deeply interesting to children, and affords infinite opportunities for investigation appropriate to all ages, through which definite ideas may be received, he made the observation of external things the basis for language work, especially in earlier years.

But the observation or study of Nature in any of her departments was never to be made for the purpose of cultivating language. That would be unnatural, artificial, direct correlation. The Nature study—botany, zöology, chemistry, or whatever the subject may be—should be studied for itself, and the language development should arise from the necessary explanation of the ideas discovered or newly revealed. Ideas naturally demand expression, and the whole work of the school should have the effect of fostering and strengthening this tendency. Ideas are only half alive if they are only conceived, and they soon die if not expressed in some form. Language should therefore be associated with every subject, and may for this reason be regarded in a sense as a correlating subject.

Froebel would correlate mathematics, too, with the study of Nature. "Man needs," he says, "a fixed point and a safe guide in the study of the inner connection of all the manifold diversity of Nature. What can furnish a more reliable and uniting starting point in this than that which appears as the source from which all diversity develops itself, the visible expression of all law and obedience to law—viz., mathematics?" "As a phenomenon of both the inner and the outer world, mathematics belongs equally to man and Nature." "Therefore it is possible to study Nature in her forms and organisms and with the help of the formulated laws of human thought in mathematics."

"Mathematics is the expression of the inner cause and of the outer limitations and properties of space. As it originates in unity, it is in itself a unity; and as space implies diversity in direction, shape, and extension, it follows that number, form, and magnitude mutually imply one another, and are an inseparable three in unity."

"Mathematics appears as a mediator between man and Nature, between the inner and the outer world."

He claimed that the study of mineralogy, geology, chemistry, physics, zoölogy, biology, botany, and even geography, in high schools, colleges, and universities must be to a considerable extent dead formalism if the proper germ centres are not formed in early childhood by intimate companionship with Nature. A true study of the sciences at maturity results from a loving appreciation of Nature's processes and a reverent recognition of the life and beauty of Nature in childhood. Interest in the life itself in early years leads in due time to a deeper interest in the origin of life and the infinite variety of its manifestations and their scientific classifications. Study stimulated by such interest is most educative, and it is likely to lead the student to original investigation beyond the limits of discovered knowledge. A really vital education does not leave a man satisfied with truth as already revealed. It arouses a greater wonder power in regard to undiscovered truth, and inspires a determination to add to the treasures of knowledge, that present happiness and future development may be more complete. Here, again, Froebel finds his loftiest interpreter, his kindred soul, in Wordsworth. After describing the joyousness of true intercourse with Nature, and the elevation of mind and spirit resulting from the recognition of her life, and majesty, and evolutionary development, he says:

. . . Science then
Shall be a precious visitant; and then,
And only then, be worthy of her name.
For then her heart shall kindle; her dull eye
Dull and inanimate, no more shall hang
Chained to its object in brute slavery;
But taught with patient interest to watch
The processes of things, and serve the cause
Of order and distinctness, not for this
Shall it forget that its most noble use,
Its most illustrious province must be found
In furnishing clear guidance, a support
Not treacherous to the mind's *excursive* power.

So build we up the being that we are;
Thus deeply drinking in the soul of things,
We shall be wise perforce; and while inspired
By choice, and conscious that the will is free,
Unswerving shall we move, as if impelled
By strict necessity, along the path
Of order and of good. Whate'er we see,
Whate'er we feel, by agency direct
Or indirect, shall tend to feed and nurse
Our faculties, shall fix in calmer seats
Of moral strength, and raise to loftier heights
Of love divine, our intellectual soul.

The visible forms of expression, writing, modelling, painting, and drawing, he would also correlate with Nature study. Writing he makes the expression of thought in visible language, so that it receives its connectedness through language as spelling and reading do. The child can not find any things more appropriate for modelling, painting, and drawing than natural objects. Froebel himself says: "To the contemplation of the external world, and especially to that of the plant world, the cultivation of the sense of colour and form, which is the introduction to drawing and painting, is closely attached." Number he associated in its first steps with these subjects, the child, for illustration, having to count the two eyes, two arms, two legs, five fingers, five toes, in drawing a man, or the six legs of a beetle, the number of petals in a flower, in drawing these objects. Thus the new revelation of the quantitative relationship as expressed by number comes to the child incidentally, and not as a formal lesson on number given with objects. The objects used by Froebel are used always for the accomplishment of a definite purpose of self-expression, and not as mere representatives of number. The lessons in number illustrated by objects, as taught by most modern teachers, are very much inferior to Froebel's elementary lessons in number. He introduced the child to number in many other ways in addition to the number work in connection with modelling, painting, and drawing. In his occupations in the kindergarten and in the work with the gifts number, form, and space concepts are constantly defined, and always defined incidentally as an essential and natural part of the work in hand.

Dr. Harris, in a report on St. Louis schools, in speaking of children in the kindergarten, says: "Geometry and arithmetic seem to unfold simultaneously in the minds of the pupils."

Geography in its elementary study is almost entirely a department of Nature study. In order to make the study intelligible to children, they must have clearly defined concepts relating to the varied forms of the earth's surface, which they have received through their own experience with mother earth. They must have a knowledge of the soil of hills and valelys, and of the influence of streams and storms on different kinds of soil. Children in cities who are without such clear concepts must be made acquainted with them by their teachers in excursions to the country or to the suburbs of the city after heavy showers; but even by this plan the necessary conceptions required as apperceptive centres can never be given so thoroughly as they are received by the child who has lived in the country always, and who has become acquainted with the features of mother earth almost as fully as with those of its own mother.

Froebel aimed to define and extend the boy's knowledge of the conditions of the earth's surface in connection with the study of botany. "Botany," he writes, "is connected in a perfectly organic way with the knowledge of the surface of the earth; for many plants are companions of the water, and grow on the border of brook and river, and give beauty to the springs of both; many plants prefer to deck the turf of the meadow and valley, and many love the clear, fresh, balmy air of hill or mountain top; many the neighbourhood of man, and many the deep recesses of the woodland; many the ocean ships bring us from distant parts of the world." Incidentally by the study of botany, or indeed any extended study of Nature, the boy becomes acquainted with the surface of the earth so thoroughly that geographical study may be properly based on the apperceptive centres in his mind.

Perhaps Froebel's strongest reason for making Nature take a prominent place in the study of childhood is its direct influence on ethical culture. As has been stated in Chapter VII, he saw in Nature the best means for revealing life, the evolution of life, and the source of life to the child. He values history and literature, if properly taught, as aids in the development of the moral nature, but he looked to sympathetic study of Nature to form a large part of the true foundation of character. Without a foundation there can be no development.

Unfortunately, Froebel was not able to organize his system above the kindergarten, so that his processes of correlation after the kindergarten period are given to us only in general theoretic statements. It is clear, however, that he would make Nature study, as Mr. Bowen beautifully expresses the thought, "take its place as the leading object, till in the school proper it becomes that *which reconciles everything and unites the growing curriculum into one organic whole.*"

Yet it is restrictive to Froebel's view of connectedness to say that he made any one subject the centre to which or through which the others should be correlated. He did not absolutely limit the mediation to one subject or department of study. In some respects he made mathematics a unifying subject. He says, "Mathematics mediates, unites, generates knowledge." The mathematical conceptions of number, quantity, form, and space are essentially connected with Nature, and help man to grasp Nature in a progressively definite and more comprehensively related way. Chemistry, geology, crystallography, physics, and all departments of Nature study relating to inorganic matter and the forces of Nature are intimately related to mathematical study, so that in a sense Froebel was right in regarding mathematics as a mediating or relating study.

He saw, too, that language should be connected with all other studies, but he considered language as the result, not as the origin of thought, and so did not regard it as a correlating element in a course of study.

In the last analysis, however, Froebel made the individual child the correlating centre. The child attends to what interests it. It learns rapidly and easily the facts and principles vitally related to its interests. Nature is the child's universal sphere of deepest interest, and through Nature or in connection with Nature there is ample scope for the interrelated, incidental development of all the powers of the human mind. But the selfhood of the child is, after all, the active, mediating influence.

It should be the original basis and source of the interest, and, as its evolution becomes more and more complete, it will, if not dwarfed, yearn for new departments of knowledge or expression or power. Froebel experienced this in his own education. Speaking of his efforts to study German literature, he says: "In this, too, it was with me as in so many other things—any influence that came before me I had either to fully interweave with my inner life or else altogether to forego its acquisition."

The child is the true psychological centre for unity in the course of study. When teachers have fully grasped this truth the studies will be presented to the child as it seeks for them to satisfy the demands of its developing nature. True self-activity will make it possible for the child to do this. In the past, and too often in the present, the teacher has not paid the slightest attention to the present needs of the child as revealed by its own manifestations of interest. Its assumed capacities, and not its real interests, have guided the teacher in deciding what it should study. Its individuality and its nascent periods, when its interests naturally centre about special subjects or forms of activity, have been ignored. Child study will in the end lead to the recognition of the sacred rights of the child in these matters. Unfortunately, the child is yet too often studied to find what the teacher can do to educate it. Froebel studied the child to learn how the teacher can aid the child to educate itself. Froebel's ideal must prevail. The teacher must become "more passive and following," less dogmatic and energetically directing.

When the child is permitted to be self-active in its

own development, its unfolding interests will be the truest guide in the correlation of studies.

Whether we believe, as nearly every one does, in simple correlation, or interrelation between studies, or in the co-ordination of unified groups, or in the concentration of all studies around one centre, we may find the origin of our thought in Froebel's writings. He may perhaps be best described as a concentro-correlationist.

He magnified the child as the basis of inner connection much more than Herbart. He insisted on the evolutionary stages of human growth as a fundamental and dominant element in all true education, and demanded such consideration for the needs of the child as would secure perfect adaptation of its studies to its stage of development. In this the best modern exponents of Herbart agree more fully with Froebel than did Herbart himself. Ziller and Rein are agreed that "the growing personality of the pupil is the centre to which all the multiplicity of interests and new ideas must be related."

This was Froebel's central thought in regard to connectedness in school work.

CHAPTER IX.

APPERCEPTION.

One of the defects that Froebel noted in the work of Pestalozzi was that he was satisfied with cultivating the power of sense perception without giving consideration to the unification of the resulting perceptions in the mind. Froebel aimed to secure the "inner connection" between the knowledge or experience of the child and the new knowledge that was brought to it by the senses, for he knew that without true relatedness, which results in a unity between the old inner and the newly revealed outer, there can be no real advance in knowledge or consequent increase in power. One of his mottoes was:

> Always, whatever with a child you do,
> Remain in touch with its own life all through.

It is doubtful whether any other educator ever saw the meaning of apperception and its importance in education as clearly as Froebel did. It is certain that no other educator discovered a law of method which necessarily secures such active apperception as Froebel's law of self-activity. That he has not received full credit for his advanced ideas in relation to correlation, interest, and apperception, is largely due to the fact that he is known to most teachers only as the founder of the kindergarten. He never could have founded a kindergarten if he had not had a profound knowledge of the fundamental principles of education. His great purpose in founding the kindergarten was to fill the child's life with the germs of true feeling and thought as a basis for its best and fullest development in later years. He saw very clearly that without these germs in the child's mind, as apperceptive centres, the proper intellectual and spiritual culture of man is impossible. He claimed that "every subject of future instruction and discipline should germinate in childhood," and he aimed in the kindergarten to provide a comprehensive and scientific system by which mothers and kindergartners could definitely aid this most essential germination by guiding the pupil's own free self-activity. He did not write books about apperception, but he is the only educator who recognised its importance so clearly as to found an elaborate and well-organized system of education to prepare all children for perfect apperceiving. He not only founded a new system of education, but he adapted it to a stage of the child's evolution hitherto untouched by educators. It is during the period before the child goes to the regular school that its mind should be stored with the germs that give vitality and productiveness to feeling and thought. The thought content of a child's mind on entering school has a most important influence on its educational development, but its influence is not comparable to that of the symbolic outlines of feeling and thought that should lie in its mind as formative elements which will spring to vigorous life at the touch of kindred feeling and knowledge during the period of its conscious education. The recognition of this great truth, and the equally important fact that the implanting of the symbolic germs of feeling and thought must be done during the earlier evolutionary stage of the child's life, and the careful working out of a definite system of education adapted to the unconscious, symbolic period of the child's development, which fills its mind with centres of intellectual and spiritual growth without making it conscious, make Froebel the greatest exponent of apperception. He revealed it in his work more than in his words. Blessed is the man who explains a great principle in words; blessed a thousand times is he who reveals a great principle as an organized force. Without the kindergarten to prepare for apperception in school, the teacher's knowledge of the need of apperception would be of little avail. The mind must be stored with what Wordsworth in his ode describes as—

> . . . Those first affections,
> Those shadowy recollections,
> Which be they what they may,
> Are yet the fountain light of all our day,
> Are yet a master light of all our seeing.

Froebel gradually advanced logically to the great step of his life—the founding of the kindergarten. He first saw that sense perception meant nothing to a child in school unless there was some germ in its mind to which the new perception could in some way be related. His law of evolution led him to see that the time for filling the child's life with formative types of feeling and thought is during the years before it goes to school. His law of self-activity taught him that the child during this period must be left free, so that its interest may increase and its selfhood develop. His judgment showed him that woman's perfect sympathy with childhood made her the natural educator of little children. And so, after years of thought and study and careful planning, he founded a system of education in harmony with all these principles, and named it the kindergarten. It is adapted to the complete evolution of the child, when the earliest efforts should be made to systematize its activities; in it the child's individuality is respected, and woman is its friend and guide; and by its processes with gifts, occupations, songs, stories, Nature investigation and Nature nurture, the child's mind is filled with the rootlets of feeling, thought, knowledge, and skill, which form apperceptive centres for a perfect development of feeling, thought, knowledge, and skill in school, college, university, and life-work. In writing about the kindergarten seven years after the first was opened, he said: "You see with what a foundation, a basis, with what a sum of living germs in the life material which he has gathered, the child passes from the kindergarten to the intermediate school. . . . All this awaits only development from unconsciousness through growing consciousness to consciousness itself, and this now is the task of the primary school."

Although he wrote no specific treatise under the name "Apperception," his definite recognition of the principle is found all through his writings, as well as in his organized system.

"Even the lucid word of the most lucid teacher frequently has no influence upon our sons, for they are asked to learn now what they should have learned in childhood with the help of our quickening explanations;

what, indeed, childhood meant they should learn almost without effort."

"We do not feel the meaning of what we say, for our speech is made up of memorized ideas, based neither on perception nor on productive effort. Therefore it does not lead to perception, production, life; it has not proceeded, it does not proceed, from life."

"We hear the sound, it is true, but we fail to get the image; we hear the noise, but see no movement."

"The school should give a conscious communication of knowledge, for a definite purpose and in *definite inner connection.*"

"It is imperative that parents and teachers should be careful to render the *inner life of their children as rich as possible.*"

"Of course words must find a response in the boy's life. The child must not be expected to give life and meaning to the words, but the words must give expression to what is already in the boy's soul and find their meaning in this."

"We should not forget, however, that instruction should start from the pupil's own life and proceed from it like a bud or sprout."

"Man understands other things, the life of others, and the effects of other powers, only in so far as he understands himself, his own power, and his own life."

"No new subject of instruction should be brought to the pupil unless he at least feels vaguely *that it is based, and how it is based, on previous work.*"

"That which follows is always conditioned upon that which goes before. I make that apparent to the children through my educational process."

"The knowledge before all things necessary for the welfare of future generations is that the human mind is choked in the germ by the burdensome crowd of notions *heaped up and patched on foreign to it,* rooted in nothing within."

"The child must first *be* something before he can turn to the contemplation of strange things *not wholly akin to his nature.*"

Froebel's plan for making the outer inner was by making the inner outer. In other words, he taught that the inner should be active in its use of the outer, in order to make the inner greater by the perfect assimilation of the new outer. Therefore his universal process of self-activity solved for him the problem of apperception. Having stored the mind with the varied and active formative elements of feeling, thought, knowledge, and skill in the first stage of the child's training, it was ready to proceed with the culture of these elements in school.

But he realized that it was quite possible to have in the mind the germ centre of knowledge corresponding to the new knowledge to be communicated, and to have the perceptive powers well trained without securing an increase in the amount of knowledge already gained. Knowledge must be related to other knowledge already in the mind if it is to be retained as a vital addition to our present store. Therefore it is essential not only that there shall be knowledge in the mind to which the new information may be related, but this knowledge in the mind must be aroused so that it is ready to apperceive the new information. The more active the knowledge already in the mind becomes, the more complete the fusion of the old and the new will be. Their perfect assimilation should be the teacher's aim. In true self-activity the inner centre already developed must be *actively* alert, because, led by interest, it becomes the *originating* power to arouse the activity. Self-activity requires positive, vital interest as a motive, and a much more *aggressive* attitude of the inner to the outer, the old to the new, than any form of responsive activity. By making self-activity an organic part of his educational work, therefore, Froebel made it imperative that the mind of the learner should be in the most favourable condition, and the process of learning should be the most thorough for securing perfect apperception. The spontaneous interest of a self-active child in the subject under consideration necessarily arouses the corresponding elements in the mind, and prepares them for perfect fusion with the new related elements.

Self-activity alone forms a sound basis for complete apperception, because it alone demands such vitality of interest in the mind of the learner as will lead to positive and voluntary action to gain the new information or solve the new problem. Increase of knowledge under such conditions does not result from aggregation, but from thorough assimilation, and the resultant unity is characterized by energetic vitality and by an aggressive alertness in regard to the still unconquered and unassimilated outer knowledge. This not only keeps interest in the outer alive, but makes it increasingly vigorous as a propelling inner force. True interest is not merely willing to receive knowledge; it urges on to the earnest effort to acquire it. If the outer and the inner are to become one, if the subjects and methods of the schools are to aim to modify what is *within the child,* it requires little argument to prove that the chief agent in making the transformation should be the inner itself. It alone can be a sure guide in determining what phase of the outer corresponds with the present development and attitude of the inner. Questioning may aid the teacher in forming an estimate of the kind of external knowledge best adapted to the child's stage of development and of mind-storing; but at best such an estimate is only an approximation. There is but one unerring guide, and that is unwarped and undwarfed interest, unchecked in its stimulation of self-activity. Teaching that is not directly related to the child's inner life, adapted to its stage of evolution and its culture epochs, and in harmony with the demands of its immediate interests, is of little value, and may do much harm. The true growth of the mind is effected by its being allowed to assimilate the kind of knowledge it needs, the kind adapted to its *present needs.* Self-activity seeks the right kind of knowledge to satisfy the demands of interest, which is the concentration of the present needs of the child clamouring for satisfaction, and it immediately assimilates the new knowledge into its selfhood and transforms it into character. Mr. Bowen says in this connection: "Nothing which does not spring directly from the natural primary outfit of the child—which is not a natural outcome of it—should be imported into the child in the first stage, nor indeed in any stage to which it does not naturally and rightfully belong."

A great deal of the information given in school never truly becomes knowledge. It becomes knowledge really only when it is understood in itself and its inner connection so thoroughly that it can be used, *and has been* used. This is the only complete apperception, and Froebel's law of self-activity is the only educational process that requires the fulfilment of these conditions by the pupil in learning.

A mind trained in harmony with Froebel's conception of apperception grows to be an organic unity. All knowledge to such a mind has such varied relations that it stimulates the growth of the complete mind. The more widely inner connection is established in the mind between the facts assimilated, the more interesting and the more comprehensively stimulative to productive effort they become.

Froebel applied the principle of apperception very broadly and definitely in regard to the training of the moral and religious nature. "If it were possible," he says, "that a human being could be without religion, it would also be impossible to give him religion." "Religious instruction can bear fruit, can affect and influence life, only in so far as it finds in the mind of man true religion, however indefinite and vague." The formative elements must be in the *nature* of the child. If the apperceptive moral and religious centres are not there, the ears are necessarily deaf and the eyes blind.

One of the greatest problems teachers have to solve is how to fill the minds of children before they go to school with a rich store of germs of feeling, thought, knowledge, and skill, to which the culture of the schools may be definitely related. This problem grows more important as the population of the world gathers into cities, and childhood is cut off from the information, the inspiration, the symbolic intellectual and spiritual foundations, and opportunities for constructive operations afforded by life in the country in touch with natural and objective life. The inner life must be enriched and made creative early if the work of the school is to be effective. There must be a broader real basis for the abstract. There should be no "extraneously communicated knowledge heaped up in the memory." Froebel saw the imperative need of this enrichment of childhood, and he founded the kindergarten to provide for it, in harmony with psychological principles. He aimed to fill the minds of all children with so many interconnected apperceptive centres that the infinite variety of the external might find in the inner lives the conditions of recognition and assimilation. He dreaded "cramming and ingrafting," because "God neither ingrafts nor inoculates."

CHAPTER X.

INDIVIDUALITY AND SELF-EXPRESSION.

INDIVIDUALITY or selfhood has necessarily received some attention in Chapters IV and VI, but its importance as the logical basis of self-expression demands that it be still further considered. Froebel made the complete development of the social unit the foundation for the progressive advance of organized society, and was the first educator to make this phase of the power and the importance of individuality clear.

The individuality of the child is the divinity in it, the element whose development should do most for the child and the world. The highest duty of the school is to develop the conscious personality of the child. Real personality must be an element of strength. It should be the centre of a man's character. It should be his contribution to the general character of the race. Millions fail in life because they are never clearly conscious of their own personal power. Every individual failure retards the race. This is the true basis for the value of individuality. The revelation of the strength of selfhood as an element in the general strength of humanity leads to true self-reverence and self-faith. A man who has self-reverence and self-faith rarely fails. He uses the intellectual power he possesses. A man with moderate intellectual powers and well-developed self-faith usually accomplishes more for himself and humanity than the man who has great intellectual power but little self-faith. It is not possible to give all children great intellectual power, but it is possible for the school to make each child as it grows to maturity conscious of its own highest power, and to give it faith in itself because of its consciousness of that power.

True self-reverence and self-faith are the opposites to vanity and conceit. Self-reverence and self-faith are strengthening and ennobling. They are the elements in character that lead men to do and dare and struggle hopefully. He who is sure he can not succeed has already failed. He who has a reverent consciousness of power in his own personality, and has gained the faith that springs from this consciousness, succeeds always. He does not wait for opportunities, he creates them; he is not forced to act by circumstances, but moulds circumstances and conditions.

So long as a child or man lacks respect for the product of his own best effort, his power does not increase rapidly even by use. Self-deprecation may neutralize the beneficent influence of activity or exercise of function. Faith in one's own power strong enough to lead to its use, and respect for the product of effort honestly made, give every conscious effort a widening and strengthening influence on character. Therefore the development of individuality should be one of the main purposes of every teacher.

The schools have definitely aimed to make the children as much alike as possible. They should really be made as unlike as possible, so far as the freeing of their individuality from constraint tends to make them unlike. All true harmony results from the unity of dissimilarity. No two trees or flowers are exactly alike. It would be a pity to have them so. The higher the organization the greater the capacity for variation. Men should see truth from different standpoints, and transform insight into attainment with widely varied powers. Each new view of truth, when revealed by an undwarfed individuality, gives new form or tone to revealed truth. The schools have made mixed characters, part child and part teacher. They have developed self-consciousness which is paralyzing, instead of selfhood which is strengthening and invigorating. Very few children are allowed to be their real selves, and "live their souls straight out." Men have dreaded the depravity of the child so much that its divinity has not been allowed to grow. In attempting to restrict depravity the light of the divinity in the child has been shadowed, and lives of gloom and stagnation have resulted instead of lives of brightness and advancement.

Each child should feel, when it leaves school or college, that it has some special power that must be used if the progress of the world is to be as rapid and as complete as it should be.

Froebel's lofty ideals of individuality may be gained from a few extracts from his writings:

"It is the destiny and life-work of all things to unfold their essence. . . . It is the special destiny and life-work of man, as an intelligent and rational being, *to become fully, vividly, and clearly conscious of his essence*, of the Divine effluence in him, and therefore of

God; to become fully, vividly, and clearly conscious of his destiny and life-work; and to accomplish this, to render it (his essence) active, to reveal it in his own life *with self-determination and freedom.*"

"The Spirit of God and of humanity is revealed most purely and perfectly by man if he unfolds and represents his own being as much as possible *in accordance with his individuality and personality.*"

"The child should neither be partly chained, fettered, nor swathed, nor, later on, spoiled by too much assistance."

"*Every human being has, indeed, but one thought peculiarly and predominantly his own,* the fundamental thought, as it were, of his whole being, the keynote of his life-symphony, a thought which he simply seeks to express and render clear with the help of a thousand other thoughts, with the help of all he does."

"Only in all-sided, natural, and rational development of himself and his spiritual power man finds his welfare and the welfare of mankind, and every other course hinders the true development of mankind."

"We do great violence to boy nature when we repress and supplant these normal, many-sided mental tendencies in the growing human being; when, in the belief of doing a service to God and man, and of promoting the future earthly prosperity, inner peace, and heavenly salvation of the boy, we cut off one or the other of these tendencies and graft others in their places."

"An education which does not try to raise roses from thistle bushes will wisely use all talents and dispositions, and bring each man into his proper place, out of which he will not desire to go."

"I will protect childhood that it may not, as in earlier generations, be pinioned as in a strait-jacket, in garments of custom and ancient prescription, that have become too narrow for the new time. I shall show the way, and I hope the means, *that every human soul may grow of itself out of its own individuality.*"

His great aim was "to allow a tree of life to germinate in each one's own heart, and a tree of knowledge in each one's own mind, taking care for its beautiful unfolding, that it may bring forth fresh and healthy flowers and ripe fruits."

He was anxious for individual development as the source of race development. "All progress, all culture," he said, "is the result of the *original creativeness* of the minds of every age, which have been able to increase the sum of existing intellectual and material wealth by producing something new. The imitators in a generation who allow themselves to be satisfied with what they have found at hand, and live and do only as they have been accustomed to do, can never bring about such an enrichment of civilization."

He never aimed to develop individuality for the sake of the individual alone, but aimed to qualify each man to fill the special place he was intended to occupy in the organic whole of humanity. He saw the perfect individual as more than an isolated unit. "In every human being, as a member of humanity and as a child of God, there lies and lives humanity as a whole; but in each one it is realized in a wholly particular, peculiar, personal, unique manner." This broad view of the perfect individual cleared his vision in regard to individualism and socialism, and gave him a logical basis for his theory of evolution. The race-including individual forms a perfect combining element in the all-comprehending unity of the race. Gaining strength as an individual from the cumulative development of the race, he in turn adds strength to the race. As the coral insect raises its rock by its death, the truly developed individual raises humanity by his life.

Froebel recognised in the universal desire of childhood to help in the work going on around it a race tendency to work in co-operation with its fellows; and he repeatedly warned parents and teachers against discouraging, rebuffing, or checking this very important instinct. Creativeness alone is a great power, but co-operative creativeness is a much higher ideal. The true ideal in human education is creativeness fostered and developed by self-activity in as varied departments as possible, and with the general aim of aiding in universal upward progress. With such an education in home and school, it could never be said of children as it can too commonly be said now: "When this child was small and could not help, it busied itself about everything; now that it knows something and is strong enough, it does not want to do anything." It is a serious charge against our systems of child training that, although children are born with a desire to help, they have lost this desire by the time they have acquired the power to be helpful.

Teachers should therefore aim to develop the child's individuality while bringing it into contact with the great stores of knowledge in Nature and in books, that it may become conscious of the divine essence in its nature, and reveal it to others. Teachers may weaken the child's individuality by overshadowing it by the domination of their own personality, by overdirecting it, by making it *consciously* imitative, by giving it too much assistance, and, more than in any other way, by failing to provide sufficiently varied opportunities for the exercise of selfhood in complete self-activity in the acquisition and use of knowledge adapted to its stage of development. The child's self-determining character can not develop properly; indeed, its development is scarcely possible, if the teacher is the determining agent, if it is trained to imitate deliberately, or if its own activity is prevented either by having its work done by the teacher, or by lack of appropriate work to lead it to interested self-activity.

The child's individuality is usually dwarfed before it comes to school. Few parents recognise their child's individuality sufficiently to stand reverently aside and let it spontaneously climb toward the light. Froebel said: "Every child brings with him into the world the natural disposition *to see correctly what is before him*, or, in other words, the truth."

The most unfortunate children are those whose untrained nurses or mothers foolishly do for them what they should do for themselves, and point out to them the things they should see for themselves. The child is seriously injured by such treatment. It is trained to believe that its function in the world is to demand and receive attention, and it inevitably becomes imperious, weak, and selfish. Its own power to see new things is lessened if mother or nurse leads it from scene to scene, pointing out each new attraction. "See, darling!" may prevent the development of the child's power to see independently. No power reaches its best development in any way but by the self-activity of the power itself. The power of seeing does not lie in the eye alone. It depends chiefly on the mind. Thousands of beautiful pictures are formed on the eye that are not seen. The mind sees only those pictures which it selects from the vast number in the ever-changing gallery of the eye. The power of selection and definite examination is the one that should be trained. It acts automatically in relation to those things that are of real interest, and continues to increase in quickness and definiteness unless it is dwarfed by the substitution of some other agency to do its work. In such a condition power always grows less. Training in seeing new things quickly and accurately does not modify the power, or condition, or even the activity of the eye to any considerable extent; it does influence the power of attention, and makes the mind more active and more investigative along the lines of predominant interest.

The mistake of most parents and teachers lies in assuming that they should not only present the attraction to the child's mind, but also arouse and direct its attention. Whenever this is done by any agency except the child's own self-active interest its power of attention is weakened. The duty of the guide of the child is to place it in conditions of interest to it, and allow its own mind to do its own seeing. The child's environment, and not the teacher or parent, should stimulate its mental activity.

It is a common practice to arouse children from reverie under the impression that they are mentally inactive. This is a grave error. In this way mental operations of great importance are interrupted and sometimes checked for ever. Such thoughtless interference may close windows of the soul that may never be reopened, and break silver threads that may never be reunited. Whether the child appears to be interested in its environment or not it arrests the development of its own self-active interest to direct its attention to the thing which is interesting to the adult friend who accompanies it. When the child is doing wrong its interest centre should be changed, but the child should not be conscious of the interference of the guide who leads to the change. Demanding a change of interest is a gross wrong, suggesting a change because parent or teacher has found something attractive to himself is unwise; but leading to a new interest because experience has proved it to be adapted to child development is highly commendable.

The greatest intellectual power is interest in our environment. Every child whose faculties are in a normal condition has this power naturally. If it be not impaired by the interference of adults, this power will increase in propulsive influence as the child grows older. As it is the greatest intellectual power, *it is therefore* capable of most unlimited development. It should be the revealer of all new things to the mind—new specimens, new problems, and new relationships. If allowed to perform its proper function in a natural way, it gains in awakening and directing power as the child grows older.

No two children should be attracted by exactly the same things or combinations of things in a walk in the country, or in any other gallery of varied interests. The special selfhood of each child sees in the outer what corresponds to its developing inner. The individual power to see in the outer that which is adapted to the development of the inner at present most active is the arousing source of all true interest. When a parent or teacher substitutes his own interests for those of the child, the child's interest is weakened and made responsive instead of self-active. The real life of interest dies, and teachers, after killing it, make energetic and often fruitless efforts to galvanize it into spasmodic responsive action. Individual self-active interest should be allowed to act without interference. The teacher should provide the conditions of interest by bringing them to the child or guiding the child to them. The child should do its own seeing, as the result of self-active and not responsive interest.

Mother and father are no doubt essential aids to the child in its happy and progressive growth. They are needed by the child to assist in the solution of the more difficult of its self-discovered problems, and in carrying to a successful issue some of its many plans and experiments. The child's power of insight is at first greater than its power of attainment. It sees problems that it can not solve, and it makes plans which it is not able to carry out alone. It takes its unsolved questions to mother, whom it loves, and in whose wisdom it has faith, and she has many opportunities to unfold to it the mysteries of life and growth and relationship that have been dimly outlined in its opening mind. Children have been named "Question boxes" and "Interrogation points" because they ask for explanations of so many questions. They do not, however, submit all their problems to their friends for solution. They solve most of their own problems, and only bring to their friends those for which they can not find satisfactory answers themselves. They should be encouraged to bring their unsolved problems to their friends, and great care should be taken in giving simple, clear, and complete answers to their questions, or in guiding them in finding the answers themselves, when it is possible for them to do so.

They should receive similar encouragement and as prompt and sympathetic co-operation when they come with plans which they can not work out or experiments which baffle them. Fathers have no better opportunities to establish the true relationship between their children and themselves, and at the same time to aid in developing in them creative productivity—one of the most essential elements in strong and useful character—than are afforded when their children come to them with plans or experiments which they can not complete without help. Whoever helps a child to accomplish its purposes and prevent the failure of its plans by performing the mechanical work beyond its powers, or by revealing to it new mechanical processes which it can itself apply, aids in its true development. He does more: he prevents discouragement and the weakening of individuality. The child's nature rebels at failure to accomplish its plans. Nature always protests against a violation of her laws until frequent violation has shown that her protests are unavailing. The child is at first made irritable by the failure of its plans, but every successive failure leads to greater discouragement, until at length discouragement produces paralyzing indifference, and destroys the alertness and originality of the mind. If plans are not executed, selfhood will ultimately cease to plan. During the time that the child's power to execute independently is weaker than its power to plan, co-operative help from parents or teachers is stimulating to individuality, and helps to develop the desire of the child to co-operate with its seniors when it is able to do so.

Parents and teachers should learn to preserve the natural wonder power of children, and provide conditions for its fullest development. School methods have unfortunately substituted suggestion for spontaneity, and rendered it unnecessary, if not impossible, for the pupils to develop their own natural power of self-acting interest. Self-active interest is the only true interest. It alone makes man an independent agent, capable of progressive upward and outward growth on original lines. It alone stimulates the mind to its most energetic activity for the accomplishment of definite purposes. It alone produces the complete co-ordination of the sensor and motor departments of the brain. Self-active interest is the natural desire for knowledge acting with perfect freedom, the divinely implanted wonder power unchecked by restriction and undiminished by the substitution of the interests of others. True self-active interest is the essential motive to intellectual activity and to the fullest apperceptive increase in knowledge.

The development of self-active interest is clearly the highest ideal of intellectual education. The first principle underlying the development of this power is the principle that underlies all growth: self-activity, spontaneity in the use of the power. The teacher's duty in the development of any power in his pupils is first to provide appropriate opportunities for the exercise of the power, and, second, to prevent the substitution of other agencies for the power to be developed. The true self-active interest of the child can not be developed unless it is placed in conditions of interest appropriate to its age and experience, and allowed to manifest choice in the expression of its interest. The child's self-active interest receives little increase in power or activity by acting in response to the instruction of the teacher. The teacher is responsible for providing the conditions of interest, and for aiding in the revelation of the attractiveness of these conditions in life, or action, or growth, or constructive possibilities, or beauty of form, colour, or sound, or by combinations of these elements of interest. He can not devote too much attention to the conditions of interest, but he should not try to dominate the interest of the child.

It should not be necessary even to direct attention or suggest interest directly by words. Interest is a natural power of the mind which possesses in itself the elements of progressive growth. It goes out spontaneously in the case of each individual toward those things which correspond to his mental development. It is the elementary agency in mental growth, and its power and intensity increase as mental growth becomes more definite and more complete. It is naturally self-active, and it retains this quality unless the direction of another interferes with its spontaneity. The weakening of this self-active interest is one of the most direct ways in which intellectual development can be checked.

It must not be understood that the teacher has no function in arousing interest. There are many ways in which he should stimulate the child's interest. He is responsible for the selection of the appropriate environment of material for operation or investigation to suit different ages and degrees of development. His mature judgment should present knowledge in proper order so that the child may study the various departments of knowledge at the time it is naturally interested in them. He should cultivate his own powers of illustration, narration, and exposition, that his necessary oral explanations may always be brief, definite, interesting, and stimulating to individual investigation by the pupils. Whatever he can do to make the external environment of the pupil interesting to his inner mental life should be done. The practice that should be avoided most carefully is interference with the action of the inner mental life of the pupil. Such a practice is unnatural, and prevents the development of spontaneous, self-active interest power. Interest that is led out or carried out never develops much intensity, energy, endurance, or individuality.

All "stamping and moulding" processes in education Froebel strongly objected to. Any education that was mere overlaying, or cramming in from the outside, met with his determined opposition. Education to him was the assimilation of the outer by the self-activity of the inner.

Individuality may be weakened by exercising the child's conscious reasoning power too soon, and by failure to sympathize with its imaginative nature. We should never laugh at its odd fancies nor fail to show sympathetic appreciation for its earliest literary or artistic efforts.

The true influence of education on the individual to be educated is the revelation of his individuality to himself, and the development of his own power of self-determination. To make a boy conscious of his own power, and of his self-determining power to control it, lays the foundation for his highest happiness and most perfect success in life.

The secret of the complete development of selfhood is the law of self-activity, one of the most important departments of which is self-expression. There is exactly the same wide difference between expression and self-expression that has been pointed out between activity and self-activity in Chapter IV. Expression that does not express the self in art, or literature, or oral reading, or recitation usually arrests the development of selfhood or individuality.

One of the commonest fallacies in the list of educational theories is "expression leads to self-expression." Expression and self-expression are the results of two entirely different intellectual operations. The powers of expression need culture, but they receive their best culture in expressing selfhood. Self and expression should not be divorced. Self should never be sacrificed to expression, or spontaneity and originality will be lost. The methods of training expression in the schools of the past have prevented the full development of individuality.

"My pupils write so much alike that you can hardly see any difference between their copy-books," says a proud teacher. Empty boast! Such a result means injury to the development of the individuality of every pupil. Writing should be more than mere letter formation. Our ideal in writing should be to train a free hand to move automatically in harmony with a free mind. Children have been trained to draw letters, not to write.

We have sacrificed freedom to form, and then vainly hoped for the freedom. We have restricted spontaneity by limiting lines, by direction lines, and by faint letters to be traced. We have cramped the fingers and confined the free movement of the arm, and the cramping and restriction have reacted on the souls of the children. We have made our pupils slow copyists and slavish imitators of writing; we should have given power to express thought rapidly on paper. The two elements in good writing are free rapid movement and accurate letter formation. We have striven for the second at the expense of the first, and in doing so we have weakened the character of the race.

Copying headlines, like all conscious imitation, tends to make a race of copyists, of unreasoning imitators, who live and die in bondage to those who assume the right to do their thinking for them. The time must come when there shall be no more mere copying in learning to write; when writing shall be, in mechanical execution as well as in thought expression, the representation of conceptions defined in the mind of the child, not of form conceptions defined on paper by some other person. The true test of writing is not the writing done while the mind is concentrated on the writing itself, but the writing done while the mind is filled with original thought which has to be expressed in written form. Copying subordinates individuality, and prevents the true conception of the independence and responsibility of the human soul. All conscious imitation, even of good, is weakening.

Imitation by unconscious childhood is the process by which the self-activity of the child is evolved from the instinctive bodily movements made by the child to define its muscular powers and lay the foundation for brain and neurological co-ordination. But there is a vast difference between unconscious and conscious imitation. The former is natural and helpful; the latter is certain to weaken individuality and character. As the human race rises to higher planes it loses the tendency to imitate. The schools should help men to rise by climbing, not by holding on to some one else. We should not be satisfied with any teaching process based on imitation.

It is wrong to make the child express our matured conceptions of the form of any object. It should express its own mental picture, not ours. Its power to express by hand, or tongue, or face, or gesture, is weakened every time it tries to express what it does not clearly conceive. Its power to express its individual self is weakened every time it attempts to express the conception of anybody else. Such a course destroys the harmony that should exist between conception and representation, and loss of harmony always means loss of power. The crude lines made by a child to represent a bird, a worm, a flower, a man, or a horse, may suggest no picture to our minds, but they are realities to the child who made them. A child's efforts to express its own, not some other person's conceptions, defines its conceptions, and clearer conceptions give greater power of expression.

The fettering of spontaneity and individuality by divorcing self from expression in the use of language, especially in bad methods of teaching oral expression, has been more destructive of individual power than even the methods of training in expression with the hand.

Language, according to Froebel, should be "*the self-active outward expression of the inner.* It is the expression of the human mind, as Nature is the expression of the Divine mind." Both in schools of elocution and in public schools expression has taken the place of self-expression. No one can ever regain his highest power to express his own thoughts who was forced into formalism by bad methods of teaching oral reading when a child. There can be no method by which young children can be kept for years expressing the thoughts of others in the language of others without arresting the development of self-expression. Oral expression should be an ever-growing power. Men possess more power of oral expression in childhood than in maturity; more freedom, more naturalness, and less self-consciousness. This most unsatisfactory result must be brought about by improper methods of teaching. Oral expression would keep pace with the growing soul if it were developed as self-expression, and not as the expression of the thought and language of others.

Nearly all training in oral expression given in the schools has been limited to oral reading, yet oral reading is the least developing form of oral expression. As practised in the past, it has made men weaker than children in the essentials of good oral expression. It is another illustration of the deterioration of strengthening self-consciousness into weakening self-consciousness through improper methods.

Oral self-expression has received very little attention yet, even in the most advanced schools. It is the only form of oral expression that gives complete development to selfhood or individuality. "Allowing the thoughts of others to run through our minds is not thinking." Expressing the thoughts of others in the language of others has little if any beneficial effect on the thought or self-expression of the child. As usually practised it is injurious in its influence, because it interferes with thought concentration, it weakens the natural power of self-expression, and develops weakening self-consciousness. Even where oral self-expression has been introduced into schools, teachers usually prevent complete self-expression by assigning the subjects for the pupils.

In most schools, however, the methods at present in use develop the form or means of expression without aiming to develop the individuality that should be expressed, and that should give life and impressiveness and originality to the expression. In all forms of representative expression, modelling, painting, drawing, etc., the pupils have been trained to imitate the representations of others, instead of revealing their own inner life of thought and feeling. Even dramatic expression has been taught by mechanical rules describing attitudes and facial expressions to correspond with the various conditions of thought and shades of feeling. These processes, by which teachers attempted to teach expression from without instead of from within, led to simulation, not stimulation, to formalism and hypocrisy instead of true vitality of character. The soul, the selfhood, the individuality was not trained.

The expression of original thought has not yet received due attention in connection with either written or oral language training. The great aim should be thought expression in both cases. Care should be taken to guide the child to new and richer departments of thought. The inner should be stored and enriched, and its enrichment is the surest way to enrich and beautify the language. Clear, strong thoughts never lack expression. Henry Irving was right when he said to the Harvard students: "If you are true to your individuality, and have great original thoughts, they will find their way to the hearts of others as surely as the upland waters burst their way to the sea."

Froebel said: "Works of high art" (in any department—literary, artistic, or constructive) "are always representations of the most individual, the most personal inner life of the artist." The work of every man and woman would be of a higher character if the schools paid more attention to the development of the individual inner life of each child.

After describing the folly of allowing children to grow up without enriching their inner lives, their minds and spiritual natures, and of substituting for pure symbolic development and Nature contemplation "crude, dead, heartless words," he says: "And nevertheless we expect our children, who have grown up so barren and empty of feeling, to understand poets and Nature at a later period. Then the drill-master's art—even in our day and with the children of cultured parents—is expected to impart its elocutionary tricks. Behold the poor child, vain and trembling, conceited or timid, reciting his piece, and say who is most to be pitied, the child, his teacher, the poem, the poet, or the audience."

The following is written in the same spirit: "It would prove a boon to our children and a blessing to coming generations if we could but come to see that we possess a great oppressive load of extraneous and merely external information and culture, that we foolishly seek to increase this from day to day, and that we are very poor in inner knowledge, in information evolved from our own soul and grown up with it. *We should at least cease making a vain display of the thoughts, the knowledge, and even the feelings of others.*"

The development of individuality in humanity is the true basis for universal freedom. It alone can make men independent, and no man can be free till he is independent, till he is self-respecting and self-determining. Diesterweg, in writing on behalf of Froebel, said: "What might not be the consequences if the dominion of acquired dead notions, and that intellectual servitude which has been propagated from generation to generation hitherto, could be completely banished?" To make man worthy of freedom was Froebel's aim. This element in his work alarmed the Prussian Government so that it proscribed the kindergarten in order to prevent the spread of liberal ideas regarding individual independence. It did not know that Froebel's greatest ideal was unity or community, and that by his educational system he was not only making men worthy of freedom, but at the same time laying the only logical foundation for harmony between individualism and socialism.

Teachers should remember that the destruction of individuality is most complete when the child is most constantly guided by the teacher. Closely graded schools are more likely to weaken selfhood than rural schools. The country boy is free for a considerable part of each day, even in school, from the teacher's direct interference, so that his individual efforts are not constantly checked.

Individuality may be restricted by school programmes. Programmes have been too narrow and too abstract, especially in primary classes. The programmes should be wide, because there can be no learning without attention, no attention without interest, and no general interest can be awakened and sustained without a variety of subjects for study and work. All children are not interested in the same subjects. Attempts to force a child to be equally interested in all subjects weaken its power of attention. The programme should be wide enough to stimulate each child to interested effort on the lines of its highest individual power. It is only when so working that man's growth is as definite, as rapid, and as harmonious as it should be. "Blessed is the man that hath found his work," said Carlyle; "let him ask no other blessedness." When a child's life runs along the channel of its greatest individual power all the other springs of power in its being flow into that channel, its life becomes broader and deeper, and its current stronger as the years pass away.

The worst schools are those in which there is least self-activity in working out realizations of original conceptions by the pupils. No teaching should be allowed to end with the acquisition of power. Power should be applied. Control should be exercised by the teacher in the production of the varied powers that enter into the characters of all well-trained men and women; spontaneity should be unrestricted in the use of these powers by each individual in the execution of his own plans. In the development of the universal elements of character power the trained teacher finds his true place, but in the unfolding of individual character the wisest and most loving teacher should reverently stand with uncovered head to watch the development of the Divine. The teacher may cultivate power, and may stimulate effort by supplying the conditions of growth, but independent activity alone can give life and vigour and progressive expansion to individual character.

All methods of developing self-expression from without are barriers to real spontaneity. In elocution or oral expression, for instance, the almost universal plan of giving mechanical rules for emphasis and inflection, specifying the tones of voice or gestures to be assumed to represent the feelings, or prescribing the facial expressions to be made to simulate passions, develops formalism and hypocrisy, not soul growth. The soul should dominate the body, and the attempts to make the body respond to or suggest thoughts or feelings that have no real existence in the individual consciousness helps to destroy the real power of body, mind, and spirit. The body may be made erect, graceful, active, and the voice may be made full, rich, elastic, pure, by careful training; but by far the most important training is that which cultivates the mind and heart and accustoms them to the natural control of body and voice. All kinds of training in self-expression are wrong that devote attention directly to the expression more than to the self of the pupil.

The highest destiny of each human being is the revelation of the Divine essence within him, the conscious unfolding of his individuality. Education should aid man in the accomplishment of this high destiny. All education that makes children conscious imitators, that assumes to create interest, that forces the development of any power too early, that substitutes words for definite conceptions, that stamps and moulds to pattern, and that tries to educate from without instead of from within, weakens selfhood and prevents the achievement of man's true life purpose. Froebel said, "All that does not grow out of one's inner being, all that is not one's own original feeling or thought, or at least awakens that, oppresses and defaces the individuality of man instead of calling it forth;" and again, "The instruction *forced upon the child's mind,* which does not correspond to its inner stage of development and its measure of power, *robs him of his original view of things,* and with it of his greatest power and capacity to impress *the stamp of his own individuality* upon his being."

Rousseau expressed part of this great thought when he wrote, "Every truth given too early by words plants the seeds of vice in the childish soul."

Individual powers may be trained to activity without developing the individuality. Whenever the individual is developed in operative power, and not in originating and directing power, true individuality is enslaved. Its proper functions are usurped by the teacher's personality.

Mrs. Browning, who among the poets had the most definite revelation of individual responsibility, makes Aurora Leigh, in refusing to marry the man whom she dearly loved on the conventional condition of the absorption of her life-work in his, say:

> . . . You forget too much
> That every creature, female as the male,
> Stands single in responsible act and thought,
> As also in birth and death.

And, when parting from him, she said, recognising that individuality was more sacred than even love:

> . . . I go hence
> To London, to the gathering place of souls,
> To live mine straight out.

Mrs Browning aimed to make Aurora Leigh the strongest, truest type of female character revealed in literature. The central element of power in her character she made a reverent recognition of her power and duty. Undwarfed by early tyranny, free in childhood from the coercion of a dominant soul, her soul became no incongruous mixture, but remained its own real self as it developed. To such souls God always speaks clearly. She heard his word and lived it. She saw his glory and revealed it. She felt his power and reproduced it. She recognised the divinity in her own life as her individuality, and she was true to it, and "*lived her soul straight out.*"

Froebel's ideal of individual evolution from within is the surest hope of the evolution of humanity to purity and strength. The inner must be the centre from which the life power springs.

> The Christ himself had been no lawgiver,
> Unless he had given the life too with the law.

The growth of individual inner life by originative and directive self-activity is a vital law in education. Whatever there is of duty, of purity, of holy aspiration in the child's soul should be helped to grow. Soul growth must be from within. Emerson was right in saying, "Though we travel the world over to find the beautiful, we must carry it with us or we find it not."

The child is full of holy aspirations. Lead these aspirations out, and everywhere in the wondrous world they will find corresponding beauty, whose enjoyment will prepare them for the appreciation of supernal glories that throughout the universe await the recognition of a higher spiritual insight. Each young heart has a thousand strings that should pour forth enrapturing harmony forever. Break none of the strings. Dare not to play on the wonderful instrument. No other hand can reveal its melody but the hand of the child itself.

CHAPTER XI.

OBJECTIVE TEACHING AND MANUAL TRAINING.

English and American teaching is weaker in its use of objects than in any other department of school work. Pestalozzi's aim in using objects so largely in his school was to develop the powers by which knowledge is received into the mind. His purpose was to make all men more comprehensively receptive, to open wider the windows of the soul, so that streams of light and knowledge might flow more freely into the mind. English and American teachers are even yet fettered by the conception that objects are to be used merely to communicate knowledge, to give clearer conceptions more easily, more quickly, more definitely, and therefore more permanently. Objects are usually brought into the classroom that pupils may learn their qualities, their origin, their construction, and their uses. Even in some of the normal schools, both in England and America, object teaching has deteriorated into mere information lessons, or "lessons on common things." Books on object teaching are in most cases classified collections of facts relating to objects, which are to be reproduced by the teacher and afterward memorized by the unfortunate pupils. Commonly but one object is used for the whole class, and it is of service only as the objective title to a dull and necessarily uninteresting and undeveloping lesson. In good schools, it is true, every child has in its hands a specimen of the object under consideration, or each pupil individually examines the object and makes drawings or models of it; but there are comparatively few schools in which objects are used for any higher purpose than to give increased knowledge of the things studied or to illustrate lessons on number, form, colour, etc.

Such lessons are infinitely better than lessons in which information is communicated by words, but they are much inferior in aim to the lessons Pestalozzi tried to give with objects. The very name "object lesson" is misleading, as it is calculated to direct attention to the object more than to the child. Whenever knowledge predominates over the development of the child in the mind of the teacher and in the plans and methods of the schoolroom, the education is defective. Knowledge is of great importance, but if it is made the dominant ideal neither the development of the child nor the communication of knowledge can reach its best limit. Pestalozzi's lessons with objects gave knowledge to his pupils, but knowledge was not their direct aim. Increase in power and activity of faculty was his ideal.

Froebel was not satisfied with Pestalozzi's use of objects. He was never satisfied with any method that had for its aim the development of receptivity alone. He knew that receptivity was but the initial step in the related sequence of receptivity, reflection, and execution; and he never forgot that, while the subordinate operations in a progressively related sequence have little if any direct influence on the development of the higher, the activity of the highest stage of any sequence must necessarily call all subordinate processes into their most complete, most natural, and most developing activity.

Froebel, therefore, made creativeness the all-inclusive mental operation, knowing that it required the exercise of the reasoning and receptive powers to be more energetic, more definite, and more productive than any subordinate operation. His friend and coworker, Barop, wrote: "The awakening of this eager desire for learning and creative activity was one of the fundamental thoughts of Frederick Froebel's mind. *The object teaching of Pestalozzi seemed to him not to go far enough;* and he was always seeking to regard man not only as a receptive being, but a creative and especially a productive one."

Froebel aimed to communicate knowledge, to illustrate abstractions, to arouse, define, and strengthen the observant or receptive powers, and to train the reflective or reasoning powers by his objective work. But he aimed to do much more than this. These are but steps leading to man's highest mental function, originality, creativity, or the revelation of individuality by productive self-expression. Froebel used material things to reveal selfhood, and the assimilation of knowledge, the increase in the power, the accuracy and the quickness of the receptive faculties, and the improvement of the reasoning powers resulted as absolutely necessary accompaniments of the creativeness.

By his gifts and occupations he provided for a most comprehensive system of arousing the child's observant powers, of giving new conceptions regarding mathematical forms and principles, of unfolding the artistic and constructive elements in the child's mind, and of defining all these developing ideals by using varied kinds of material to express in visible form its own original conceptions. How utterly insignificant is the common object work of the schools when compared with this comprehensive use of material in making the child's environment the direct agency in the development of its individuality!

His gifts were chosen with great care and wisdom to suit the unfolding consciousness of the child, to fill it with new conceptions suitable to its advancement, and to aid it in its artistic, mathematical, and simple constructive development. The occupations give productive employment to the child, and develop its inventive power, its artistic ability, and its constructive power; in short, they provide means of expression for the child's original conceptions, and reveal its inner powers to itself and its teachers.

There are many points of superiority in Froebel's objective work when compared with that done in most schools. In ordinary objective work the child is receptive, Froebel made it creative; the schools give information, Froebel gave power; the schools allow the child to see, or at best to examine, the object, Froebel allowed it to use it; the schools ask the child what it can find out about the object, Froebel encouraged it to find what it could do with it; the schools sometimes permit the child to make a representation of the object, Froebel required it to transform it into some other form as an expression of an original thought of its own; the schools are satisfied with increasing the store of knowledge, or at best with enlarging faculty power, Froebel desired the assimilation of knowledge by using it as it is acquired, and exercised the whole productive intellect; the schools bring the outer material to the inner life of the child, Froebel led the child's inner life to dominate and transform its material environment.

"The child must reproduce with matter what he has received into himself from the external world in order to understand it." Froebel did not mean by this statement that what is taken in is to be reproduced just as it is received. The statement is a condensation of his principle that receptivity alone can not make knowledge clear, that the internal must use the external before the outer becomes really a part of the inner.

Froebel gave a spiritual meaning to all material things. "It is quite a different thing," he says, "whether we look upon concrete things and facts as merely material, the things and facts serving for this or that outward purpose, or contemplate them as the outward form of spiritual contents, as the intermedium of higher truths and higher knowledge." He taught that "it is in this sense that education needs to use the material world." Teachers may not be able to comprehend this symbolic use of material things as clearly as Froebel did, but the conception of his aim in using objects should revolutionize the teaching of so-called "object lessons."

It is in the department of manual training that the schools are now gaining their clearest ideas of Froebel's use of material things for the development of the inner life of the child. Even here, as in object teaching proper, teachers have passed through the narrow utilitarian stage before reaching the educational basis for introducing manual training into the schools.

Froebel saw the need of manual training to broaden the school programme, to give the race greater skill, and to lead men to love work; but he advocated its introduction into schools for much stronger reasons. His reasons were educational, not economic or utilitarian. He valued the change wrought in selfhood more than the products of its work or the improvement in hand skill.

The intellectual and moral advantages of manual training are gradually unfolding in the minds of educators, but none of Froebel's successors have as yet taken as high ground as he did in regard to them. He made work a handmaid of religion, and believed that, if children were trained to regard work as a means of self-expression, it would always be to them a means of joy—the joy that should always spring from the accomplishment of a true inner purpose. "Early work," he says, "guided in accordance with its inner meaning, confirms and elevates religion. Religion without industry, without work, is liable to be lost in empty dreams, worthless visions, idle fancies. Similarly, work or industry without religion degrades man into a beast of burden, a machine."

"God creates and works productively in uninterrupted continuity. . . . God created man in his own image; therefore man should create and bring forth like God. The spirit of man should hover over the shapeless, and move it that it may take shape and form, a distinct being and life of its own. *This is the high meaning, the deep significance, the great purpose of work and industry, of productive and creative activity.* We become truly Godlike in diligence and industry, in working and doing, which are accompanied by the clear perception or even by the vaguest feeling that thereby we represent the inner in the outer; *that we give body to spirit and form to thought;* that we render visible the invisible."

"Primarily and in truth man works only that his spiritual, Divine essence may assume outward form, and that thus he may be enabled to recognise his own spiritual, Divine nature and the innermost being of God."

Froebel saw, too, the purely intellectual advantages of manual training. "Plastic material representation in life and through doing, united with thought and speech, is by far more developing and cultivating than the merely verbal representation of ideas. The life of the boy has, indeed, *no purpose but that of the outer representation of his self;* his life is, in truth, but an external representation of his inner being, of his power, *particularly in and through material.*"

The most important products of manual training are the invisible, not the visible. Brain making and brain co-ordination are the direct results of manual training. Nearly all school processes develop only a one-power brain. Every educational process that either communicates knowledge directly to the child or trains the child to acquire knowledge for itself, *and stops there,* develops the sensor or receiving brain power only. It matters little, so far as complete brain development is concerned, whether the knowledge is communicated by words or through real things, whether it is received from the teacher ready made or gathered by the pupil himself. If school education stops at receptivity and reflection, at the acquisition of knowledge and the development of the knowledge-gathering and reasoning powers, the motor brain remains undeveloped, and the co-ordination of the sensor and motor neurological systems remains practically uninfluenced by school education. Fortunately there are many opportunities for the development of these most important departments of brain power outside of school, but they are fewer and less stimulating in cities than in rural districts, and men are gathering in increasingly large numbers in cities. Even in the country, however, the schools should leave no important part of the child's development to chance; but there is a much greater need of manual training in cities and towns than in rural districts, not merely to give manual skill as a basis for industrial success, but to aid in the development and co-ordination of the brain. Froebel believed that a child's evolution could not be completed in perfect manhood unless it was brought in early years "under the influence of Nature, of *useful handiwork*, and of religious feelings."

Mr. Bowen claims for Froebel the fatherhood of all rational manual training, and he is clearly right in doing so. He says: "We distinctly assert that manual training, and in particular Sloyd, which have been making such marked progress on both sides of the Atlantic of late, *are direct and undeniable outcomes of Froebel's views*, and that, unless they are dealt with on Froebelian principles, they are certain to be *little better than a waste of time*." The founder of Sloyd explicitly states that he received his idea of the introduction of handwork chiefly from Froebel. Indeed, he was led to prepare his Sloyd work as a continuation of Froebel's kindergarten work, so that pupils could continue their handwork after they passed the kindergarten age.

Froebel's marvellous insight and his great logical power can be realized in no better way than by tracing the devious paths and laborious efforts of his successors in climbing slowly to the heights from which he saw the clear light of truth in regard to soul growth through self-expression by material things. The name "manual training," like the term "object lesson," has been narrowing. It has directed attention to the external instead of the inner development, to the production of things more than to the production of character. His successors caught the form of his thought without its life. In nearly every essential they have climbed painfully backward, instead of leaping upward with their faces toward the light.

Through the wilderness of "trade schools" educators gradually reached the higher ground of hand training without special association with any particular trade, but as a qualification for better work in any field of industrial life. Here they groped for a generation, and here the great body of those who have climbed at all still remain looking down instead of up.

During the last few years the most advanced leaders have seen and taught that the true basis on which the introduction of manual training into schools should rest is educational, and not economic or utilitarian. Froebel saw and taught this long ago, and his exemplification of this principle in the use of material in the kindergarten has done more than all other agencies to help others to see clearly what he saw.

Few have yet been able to follow Froebel to the mountain top from which he saw in manual training, in the constructive and transforming use of material, the revelation of the complete inner life of the child and the basis of its moral training. To Froebel we owe our limited conception of the educational value of manual training, to him we shall owe our greater enlightenment when in the coming days we shall see beyond the mists and shadows, and understand that the proper use of objects or material things not only reveals new knowledge, widens and strengthens our faculties, develops and co-ordinates our brain power, and cultivates our executive force, but that it is the operative foundation of spiritual evolution.

Educators, especially in England and America, began as far as possible from Froebel's position in the part of the school curriculum to which they assigned manual training. Froebel gave manual training in many adapted forms to the little children; his successors began by giving it to the oldest pupils in the high schools. Here, again, the development, where any has taken place, is slowly but progressively toward Froebel. Grade by grade downward manual training is forcing its way. In time men will see what Froebel saw so clearly long ago, that the developing influence of the use of material in productive self-activity is greatest in the early years of the child's evolution, and that if not begun then it can never by any possibility produce its best effects. Like all other education whose germs have not been developed in the first evolutionary stage, its later development is correspondingly weak and formal. The kindergarten will in time become the universal basis for manual training, because it uses handwork as a means of head and heart growth, and at the period in the child's life when it is most developing.

Froebel's objective work differs radically from Pestalozzi's, and from that of all Pestalozzi's followers in the way in which the child is required to express what it has learned from the objects used. Pestalozzi's children expressed their new ideas in words only. They gained ideas from objects and expressed them in words. Froebel used the object both to reveal and express new conceptions. Most teachers yet limit the use of objects to the in-taking of knowledge; their most developing use is in the out-giving of ideas. This best use of objects we owe to Froebel. Froebel was not satisfied with a revelation of the law of objective representation of ideas by constructive self-activity. He selected, constructed, and classified material of various kinds, and gave it to the child in the forms and quantities best adapted to define and express its ideas. To do this cost him years of careful study of childhood and its processes of self-revelation. Again, he showed his most distinctive characteristic of "translating psychological principles into psychological practice."

Froebel himself expressed in the following brief statement the great purposes for which he used material in his educational system: "The time has now come to exalt all work into free activity—that is, to make it intelligent action. This can only take place when the law, according to which all formative activity proceeds, is recognised and *consciously* applied, as it has been hitherto unconsciously applied. The occupation material of my method gives the means of unconscious application of the law on the children's part to rise to art in such a way as to come to their consciousness by degrees and be recognised as the guide and regulator of all formation. In no other way can human work be transformed into free activity. It can only become *intellectual* action out of what has been mere *mechanical* action when the occupation of the hand is at the same time the occupation of the mind. At the present time art *alone* can truly be called free activity, but every human work corresponds more or less with creative activity, and this is necessary in order to make man the image of his Divine Creator—a creator on his own part in miniature."

These sentences will bear careful rereading once a month.

CHAPTER XII.

EVOLUTION.

Having written largely in regard to evolution in previous chapters, especially in Chapters I and III, it is unnecessary to do more than quote Froebel's own words to unfold his conception of evolution. Like all basal laws, it is interwoven with all other truth, and has necessarily been kept in view when considering his other laws. The following quotations show what an inspiring and illuminating influence the law of evolution had in Froebel's life. It is an essential feature in his philosophy as the only possible foundation for progressive advancement in the individual and in the race. It is the true source of hope to the teacher, as it gives a logical basis for belief in man's intellectual and spiritual development.

"Man, humanity in man, as an external manifestation, should be looked upon not as perfectly developed, not as fixed and stationary, but as steadily and progressively growing, in a state of ever-living development, ever ascending from one stage of culture to another toward its aim which partakes of the infinite and eternal."

"It is unspeakably pernicious to look upon the development of humanity as stationary and completed, and to see in its present phases simply repetitions and greater generalization of itself. For the child, as well as every successive generation, becomes thereby exclusively imitative, an external dead copy—as it were, a cast of the preceding one—and not a living ideal for its stage of development which it had attained in human development considered as a whole, to serve future generations in all time to come. Indeed, each successive generation, and each successive individual human being, inasmuch as he would understand the past and present, must pass through all preceding phases of human development and culture, and this should not be done in the way of dead imitation or mere copying, *but in the way of living, spontaneous self-activity.*"

"God neither ingrafts nor inoculates. He *develops* the most trivial and imperfect things in continuously ascending series and in accordance with external, self-grounded, and self-developing laws."

"In general, whatever of human education and development has been neglected in boyhood will never be retrieved."

"Every phase of development, however beautiful and proper in its place, must vanish and perish whenever a higher phase is to appear. The sheltering bud scales must fall when the young branch or the fragrant blossom is to unfold, however much these tender forms may thereby be exposed to the rough weather of the spring. The fragrant blossom must make room for a fruit, at first sour, hard, and homely. The luscious red-cheeked fruit must decay that vigorous young plants and trees may sprout forth."

"One's own perceptions awaken one's own conceptions, and these awaken one's own thinking in later stages of development. Let us have no precocity, but natural—that is, consecutive—organic development."

"The laws of the universe are the same as the laws of human education. Kindergartens form a stage of development in the culture of man out of which the succeeding stages will follow according to a determined law, as is the case in organic life."

"Every new stage of human development which occurs in its own time as surely as the time itself comes, and like the time brings in cyclical consequence its own peculiarities, increases the capacity for the understanding of truth, and thus broadens the knowledge of God."

"Humanity, looked at externally, is not seen to be an already perfected thing, not an absolutely established, lasting thing, but a continually progressive, growing thing, rising from one stage of culture to another, striding toward the goal that touches upon infinity."

Christ said, "I am come that they might have life, and *that they might have it more abundantly.*" Froebel, since Christ, is the greatest revealer of the ideal of "more abundant life." He saw the ascending stages in God's created works, from inorganic matter, through organized life in Nature, to man and to the centre of the organic whole, God himself. He noted the progressive sequence of related stages in the growth of plant life, animal life, and man. He saw the similarity between individual man and humanity in gradually unfolding development. He believed that new revelations are made to the race and to individuals when they are made ready for the new revelation by having consciously lived up to the revelations already made. He looked for a continuously progressive ascent of the human race from one higher stage of culture to a still higher, limiting the highest only by "the goal that touches upon infinity." The duty of all men, especially of teachers, is to help the race to leap from stage to stage in its evolution toward the light.

The history of the race proves the possibility of upward development. The world moves on to a higher ground, and as it moves the light grows brighter and sight grows clearer. Old beliefs and theories and conventionalities fall away into the valley of errors. Each generation marvels at the darkness of the one that preceded it. Each man regrets his father's benighted condition, and is in turn pitied by his son. As men become more free they rise to higher stages more rapidly. There is no department of life-work in which there are fixed conditions. Scientists, doctors, teachers, statesmen, even the theologians, grow beyond their shells, and build each year "more stately mansions" for their souls, leaving "the past year's dwelling for the new."

To every man and woman Froebel said, what Holmes said so exquisitely after him:

> Leave thy low-vaulted past!
> Let each new temple, nobler than the last,
> Shut thee from heaven with a dome more vast,
> Till thou at length art free,
> Leaving thine outgrown shell by life's unresting sea.

What inspiration and hope the idea of evolution brings to the teacher! He is no longer a hearer of lessons, a teacher of words, or even a developer of power. He is a stimulator and helper of life to higher life. Middendorff said: "To tend human germs in a constantly progressive manner in every new stage of human development is certainly no mean calling, but the greatest and most important for every generation." Every teacher may climb where others never climbed. For the sake of humanity and for our own growth we should climb along new paths lighting beacon fires as we go up. The best thing we can do for another soul is to start it to climb for itself.

The rainbow rests on the crest of the mountain yonder. The pot of gold lies where the rainbow touches the hilltop. What though the glorious bow moves on to crown a higher peak as we ascend? There is joy in the fact that there is always another hill to climb with a new pot of gold at the top.

The Baroness von Marenholz-Bülow, in replying to the insinuation that Froebel's principles were in harmony with those of the revolutionary party in Germany, said: "The motto of the revolution is *overthrow,* while Froebel's motto is *development*—development of men and things."

Evolution is now one of the central ideals of education. We owe it largely to Froebel. Dr. Harris says: "Inner connection is, in fact, the law of development, *the principle of evolution,* and Froebel is the educational reformer *who has done more than all the rest* to make valid in education what the Germans call the 'developing method.'"

CHAPTER XIII.

FROEBEL'S ETHICAL PRINCIPLES.

CHARACTER building is the supreme aim of Froebel's educational system. His principles of moral and religious culture are therefore worthy of careful study.

He applied precisely the same laws to the revelation of ideals of right, justice, duty, and will that he applied in the general development of the child. The law of evolution led him to believe that the development of moral and religious ideals must be a progressive growth adapted to the expanding stages of the child's life. He never made the child a formalist or a hypocrite by forcing on it a mature theology or the conduct of an adult. The law of evolution revealed to him also the necessity for implanting in early years the formative elements of moral and religious life, and gave the inspiring conception of progressive growth to higher life. His law of unity prevented his making the blunder of dissociating the highest life of man from his common everyday experience. In this way he dignified work and made religion practical. His recognition of the sacredness of individuality made him expect a distinct moral and religious evolution for each individual. His law of community taught duty, helpfulness, and co-operation.

The law of apperception led him to see the impossibility of giving a religious training at all, unless the germs of religious feeling and thought were implanted in the child's life.

He believed the three foundation elements in a religious life to be community, love, and life. The child's earliest feelings of community and love he would have developed in the loving family life, and its unconscious basis for the conscious revelation of active, progressive, evolving life he would lead it to gain from sympathetic contemplation of Nature.

Speaking of the family, he says: "This feeling of community, first uniting the child with mother, father, brothers, and sisters, and *resting on a higher spiritual unity*, to which later on is added the unmistakable discovery that father, mother, brothers, sisters, human beings in general, feel and know themselves to be in community and unity with a higher principle—with humanity, with God—this feeling of community is *the very first germ of all true religious spirit*, of all genuine yearning for unhindered unification with the eternal, with God."

"Inasmuch as every separating tendency hinders pure human development, man, even in childhood, refers everything to family life, beholds everything through family life, as is shown so clearly in childhood."

"Pure human, parental, and filial relations are the key, the first condition, of that heavenly, Divine, fatherly, and filial relation and life of a genuine Christian life in thought and action."

"The comprehension of the purely spiritual human

relations, of the true parental and filial relations, furnishes the only key for the recognition and apprehension of the relations of God to man and of man to God."

"As long as mothers do not know how to administer the priestly office at home for their children's benefit, so long will their piety suffer."

One of his great purposes was the ennoblement of family life. He desired to make it pure, true, loving, that it might fix in the child's nature types of purity, truth, and love, and become to it an emblematic representation of perfect society and of the relationship of humanity to God. He valued the life of the home far more than any moral or religious teachings of the home, although he did not underestimate these provided they were wisely given and were suitable to the child's stage of development.

As he made family life the source of true religious *feeling*, he made Nature the book in which the child in early years can find its clearest *thoughts* of God, and receive into its mind the apperceptive germs to which may be related the most vital elements of religious thought. He speaks often and strongly on this question. He objected vigorously to the deadening practice of attempting to reveal spiritual truth or any other truth to a mind in which there are no related centres established by experience. The following thoughts are types of many others found in his writings:

"We have to open the eyes of our children, that they may learn to know the Creator in his creations. Only when they have found or divined God as the Creator through visible things will they learn to understand the 'Word of God'—God in spirit and in truth—and be able to become Christians. First is the visible world, then the invisible truth—the idea."

"The capacity for belief or sense of truth is killed out in the childish heart when the truth is presented to it only in the form of abstract language."

"By pointing out God's works while rambling through the scenes of Nature a thousand opportunities offer for worship."

The contemplation of Nature's processes should reveal God to the child as Creator, and this is the first step toward true knowledge of his being. It also reveals the element of life and of developing life, and from these the child learns to recognise the possibility of human evolution. By its nurture of the life in Nature it learns its power to improve life, and by sowing the seeds of plants it realizes that it may aid in the increase of life. These thoughts, when their time of fruitage in character arrives, enable the child to realize that it has power to help all life to higher, better, purer, truer life. This is one of the most energizing thoughts that lie at the foundation of true religious life.

The germination of a seed, the growth of a plant, the unfolding of a bud, the blooming of a flower, the structure of a leaf, the song of a bird, the love and mysteries of a bird's nest, the home-making of an insect, the evolution of a worm into a butterfly, the rippling of a brook, the vastness of the ocean, the majesty of a mountain, the movement of trees in the wind—all these Froebel uses to quicken the intellectual and spiritual life of the child. It must not be understood that Froebel expected the child to be made conscious of God by its life amid the mysteries of Nature during its unconscious stage of development. This he would deplore. The revelation of life as the unifying and evolving power in Nature was his aim. He believed that by the recognition of life in Nature and by performing all its work in the kindergarten in a logical, progressive, evolving sequence, the ideals of life and law would definitely unfold in the child's consciousness, and ultimately reveal God not only as the source of life and law, but as life and law, the all-pervading elements that give unity and progressive evolution to the universe. "Knowledge of God, like all knowledge, enters the human mind by degrees from the first presentiment up to faith, and then on to sight, till the spirit comes up into highest unity or consciousness of God."

Nature is the most sacred temple for the child. In it the child gives its truest worship, unconsciously overflowing with adoration and receiving into its life silent streams of reverence and elements of vital truth direct from the centre of life to strengthen its soul as naturally as the trees and flowers around it are nourished by the material elements that give them life and growth. What life-revealing and life-stimulating sermons are preached to it by the seed, the plant, the bud, the flower, and the worm in their evolution toward a new life! What hymns are sung to it by cricket and bee and bird! What revelations of joy and peace and majesty and glory enter its spiritual life as it lies on a June day looking beyond the floating clouds, and dimly conscious of the melody and mystery of life!

From the lips of an enraptured worshipper, who was five years old, and into whose life flowed comfort and joy and elation from the myriad sights and sounds of Nature till her heart overflowed, came with reverent sweetness the words, "Thank you, God." Her religious life was developing from within. It had no formalism, or any other element of death. It was the spontaneous expression of real feeling, and not a mere ceremonial. She felt a faith she never could have learned by words.

Froebel aimed to make mothers and teachers wise enough to train childhood so that its spiritual evolution might never be arrested. Only a few great souls carry over into their conscious life the undimmed insight, the untiring alertness, and the ever-increasing assimilating power of their spiritual natures in unconscious childhood. The best growth of humanity must be forever retarded so long as its highest power is dwarfed by weak or false training.

The loving contemplation of Nature prepares the child for the recognition of the underlying universal law of unity, and ultimately for man's greatest revelation—that he is himself subject to this same law, and responsible for bringing himself into harmony with it, that he may reach his best development as an individual, and become fully qualified for the fulfilment of his highest destiny, and do his part nobly in applying this law in the universal community of which he is an essential part.

Many scientists have made science a basis for unbelief. Froebel made it an essential part of the basis of true religion, a revealer of God; the only true revealer to the child of life, reverence for life, evolution in life, and therefore of the conception of the possibility of higher human life and of human power to aid all human life to higher life.

The Baroness von Marenholz-Bülow said, in conversation with Middendorff: "In our time men seem to have forgotten Nature in favour of spirit, and objects in favour of abstractions; the word is separated from the thing and governs, and generally, only as a mere empty word, is not understood. It is quite clear to me that Froebel's method and doctrine will reverse this process, and first connect facts with the *outer and inner experience* as their root and their cause. Thus only can the spirit of truth, which is the Spirit of God, again be recognised as one and the same in Nature and in the mind. Froebel's idea of education strives to bring to the full consciousness of men their relations to Nature (the Divine nature), and thereby must the relation of men to God (in the Spirit) and to all that is divine, as Christianity teaches, be lifted to higher and clearer recognition. *One side of truth verifies and explains the other side.*" Middendorff replied: "You are right. One truth must ever confirm another; the recognised truth will be more clearly and deeply understood through every new one discovered. The spirit of Christianity, so very much misunderstood and mistaken at present, will awaken to new life in children, and appear in a new and higher light, when Froebel's idea of education has been practically applied. This is my deepest conviction."

Froebel believed "that we may restrain the sins which spring from the animal appetite when we direct the regards of the child to something that satisfies his higher ideal or spiritual wants." These higher spiritual powers are a part of the child's nature at birth, and they need to be nourished in order that they may grow. As the body grows by receiving proper nutrition, so the spiritual nature develops if it is satisfied; as the body dies from lack of proper nourishment, so does the spiritual nature lose its vital energy unless supplied with the elements of spiritual interest. "The spiritual unconsciousness into which the child is born is changing into conscious being from the first moment of life. The incentives which are needed for the awakening of the powers of the soul go out from the external world. . . . The senses are to be awakened as the organs of the mind, and not as the organs of mere sensuous pleasure or of mere desires, as in the animals."

This was one of Froebel's great thoughts for the training of humanity. He saw that the misuse of the very elements of character that should make men pure and noble led to their degradation and debasement, and that thousands even of Christian parents prayed for the salvation of their children while they allowed them to plant in their natures the seeds of moral death. The senses are agents of the soul, and should never become the slaves of the body. When they do, sensuality takes the place of spiritual wisdom. When men and women learn to train their children properly the words of Solomon will be understood and believed by Christians, "Train up a child in the way he should go, and when he is old he will not depart from it." Many mothers deprave their children by giving them improper food; by giving their food too often, or in too large quantities; or by creating an unnatural taste for sweetmeats. This lays the foundation of self-indulgence, for the gratification of appetites that should never have been formed. Froebel saw even more clearly than Ruskin that "all evil springs from unused (or misused) good," and he yearned to make parents and teachers wise in the training of the child, so that no good of body, mind, or spirit should be unused or misused. Froebel's expression of this thought is much more comprehensive than Ruskin's: "A suppressed or perverted good quality—a good tendency, only repressed, misunderstood, or misguided—lies originally at the bottom of every shortcoming in man."

The same elements in our nature form in our lives either love or hate, calmness or passion, truth or falsehood, courage or cowardice, constructiveness or destructiveness, temperance or self-gratification, self-control or self-indulgence, selfishness or unselfishness, strengthening self-consciousness or weakening self-consciousness, purity or debasement. How supremely important it is, therefore, that humanity should study the child as Froebel did, to find how all the beautiful and the wonderful in Nature may be made to stimulate the good and not the evil in the intellectual and spiritual life of the child!

By keeping the child from its earliest years in an atmosphere of purity, joyousness, and self-activity, surrounded with the beautiful in Nature, colour, form, music, and symbolic story, Froebel believed it possible to so strengthen the good in the child's intellectual and spiritual nature that it would continue to grow and remain a controlling ethical force through life. The spiritual nature may be trained to be receptive to all pure and ennobling influences, and if these influences when received into the child's life are not merely allowed to accumulate, but are wrought into character by the creative self-activity of the child, they do a great deal to eradicate coarseness and immorality from its nature.

He did not accept the theory of the total depravity

of the child, but taught that every child has in its nature elements of divinity that when properly developed constitute the true unity between humanity and God. He believed man to be the highest created being, and he refused to believe that all his tendencies are by nature toward evil. He saw in the child elements of Divine love and power which educational forces should keep in perfect, productive, creative unity with divinity. He believed that man was created in harmony with universal unity, and that the elements of his own nature were originally harmonious. He knew that evil, the misuse of good, had partially destroyed this beautiful harmony, and he believed that the highest function of education is to restore this lost harmony.

The doctrine of total depravity he regarded as paralyzing to all human effort for self-evolution. There is little hope or inspiration in the work of a teacher who believes that he is teaching beings who are totally depraved, in whom there are no elements of purity and wisdom and progressive growth; but there is a sacred joy to him in the consciousness that each child possesses creative force and other elements of divinity, the love of that which is inherently beautiful, a capacity for love, ennobling aspirations, a mind that may grasp the problems of the infinite, and a spirit that should respond to its Creator. The teacher who holds this view of childhood believes that he is moulding creative forces, and is in the best sense a coworker with the Creator himself.

Froebel wrote very strongly against the theory of total depravity. He said: "Whoever considers that which is finite, material, physical, as in itself bad, thereby expresses contempt for creation, Nature, as such—

nay, he actually blasphemes God. It is treason to human nature and to man to consider him in his essence as neither good nor bad or evil; how much more, then, is it treason to consider him in his nature as essentially bad or evil!"

The progress of mankind religiously has been delayed by the lack of true self-reverence. Froebel was the apostle of higher self-recognition. His loving faith in the development of the good in humanity has revolutionized the teaching and disciplinary processes of progressive educators, but its best work will be done when it reveals to all men their native divinity, and makes education and life-work a conscious growth toward the Divine. True humility does not spring from a consciousness of weakness and depravity, but from the consciousness of power which reveals responsibility and relationships, and helps man to realize that he is but one of a mighty host of workers for truth. There is little development in any religion that gives to its believers the enfeebling conception that they are merely "unworthy worms." No man can have true faith in God who has not true faith in himself.

Froebel strongly objected to the defining of evil in the mind of the young child as an element in its own character. To do this necessarily degrades the child's moral sense. "It is certainly a very great truth," he says, "and failure to appreciate it does daily great harm, that it generally is some other human being, not infrequently the educator himself, that first makes the child or the boy bad. This is accomplished by attributing evil—or at least wrong—motives to all that the child does from ignorance, precipitation, or even from a keen and praiseworthy sense of right or wrong. Unfortunately, there are still such men of mischief among educators. To them children and boys are little malicious, spiteful, lurking sprites, where others see at most a jest carried too far, or the effect of too free an exercise of spirit. Such birds of ill omen, especially when they are educators, are the first to bring guilt upon such a child who, though not wholly innocent, is yet without *guilt;* for they give him motives and incentives which were as yet unknown to him."

Evil should not be defined in the consciousness and will of the child as a personal motive in its life. In this way consciousness of innocence is destroyed, and the positive character is paralyzed. Positivity is the central element in character. Knowing the will of God by doing it, and acting the defined will for humanity—this is the Christian life that meets the Divine approval. Froebel ridicules the religious training that first makes a boy believe himself bad, then coerces and restricts and dwarfs him into external submissiveness, and, finally, like the boy who has maltreated a fly and torn off its wings and feet, says, "See how tame!"

Children love to do good better than evil. Christians must believe this or they believe that God's highest created beings prefer evil to good. Such a belief prevents the conception of the ideal of progressive advancement from stage to stage by humanity and individual man. The parent or teacher should provide facilities for the child's productive occupation. If this is done the destructive tendency will gradually vanish from its character. The mother or teacher should guide to a change in the centre of interest when the child is tend-ing toward the wrong. The great dangers in the ethical training of children are the weakening of self-reverence in the immature consciousness and the consequent lack of positiveness or independent aggressiveness for truth.

The great body of Christians are negative. They need independent vitality. They wait for leadership. They depend on external stimulation, and work with spasmodic energy when electrified by the fervid enthusiasm of others. The greatest lessons taught to the world by Christ are individual power and individual responsibility. The teaching of the theologians has so far failed utterly to reveal to men a due sense of the divine power they possess, and which they should cherish and develop above all else. It is true that it has given to some men a sense of responsibility, but it is a sense of *responsibility for the evil and not the good* in their natures. The great work of the Church should be to convince man of his power to aid in the overthrow of evil and the accomplishment of good. This is the true basis of responsibility. The teaching that makes a man feel responsibility only for his sins is a blighting misrepresentation of Christ's most vital revelations.

Froebel longed to have the school, the home, and the Church work in perfect harmony in the development of the child. He aimed to make it positive, not negative; self-reverent, not self-abased. He would as long as possible prevent its recognition of evil in its own nature by directing its attention to its powers to achieve good and providing appropriate means for their exercise. The defining of the consciousness of evil must weaken character, the gradual defining of individual good by creative self-activity in executing unselfish purposes develops true character force, and helps to make the divinity in the child the dominant element in its nature.

Froebel pleaded that the child might be free from the terrorism of religious teaching. Speaking of his own experience, he says, "Great was my joy when I believed I had proved completely to my own satisfaction that I was not destined to go to hell." He was a most earnest Christian, but he wished to save the child from the "stony, oppressive dogmas of theology." He believed that the seeds of character require the sunshine of joyousness for their early germination and development, as the seeds of plants need the warmth and light of the sun; and that as plants grown in a cellar are feeble and delicate, so characters developed in gloom and fear lack vitality, strength, and positivity. He recognised a wide difference between the darkness of difficulty and the shadow of dread. Difficulties are opportunities for victory; dread palsies power. No life—physical, intellectual, or spiritual—is true life unless its highest characteristic is power. The religious or ethical training that by terrorism or in any other way weakens power, prevents the growth of divinity in humanity, and retards the progress of humanity toward the Divine.

He criticised severely the practice of associating gloom and sadness with religion and severity and punishment with God in the mind of the child. It is a deplorable thing to misrepresent God to a child; yet it has been customary for parents and even teachers to speak of God to children as a kind of malicious spirit who dislikes bad children so thoroughly that he is continually on the lookout for opportunities to punish them. They represent the loving Father as a spy ever on the alert to wreak vengeance on what they are pleased to call "naughty children." Froebel led the child to see God as love, life, and the centre of all unifying and uplifting power.

Gloom is unnatural in a child's life, and it is a fatal mistake to give it the impression that religious life, the expression of its highest nature in adoration and action, should have in it any element of melancholy or dread. The unity of Divinity with the divinity in man should bring to the awakening consciousness its highest happiness. Even the child's social and creative plays should be truly reverent worship to it. In all departments of its unfolding life happiness is a preventive of evil and a stimulus to good. The puritanical idea that associated joyousness and art and music with evil was a perversion of truth that blighted true religious culture. Froebel was one of the first to protest against it on philosophically religious grounds. The shadows of religious gloom are lifting, and the brightness of religious life will soon shine full and clear. There are few Christians now who would sympathize with the Scotchman who, after visiting Edinburgh on Sunday, said, "It was an awful sight to see the people so happy on the Lord's day."

Froebel objected as definitely to the attempts to make children love good by bribing them as he did to attempts to make them hate evil by terrorizing them. He had little faith in the piety either of child or man that rested on promises of rewards either in the present or the future. "It argues a low degree of insight into the nature and dignity of man if the incentive of reward in a future world is needed in order to insure a conduct worthy of his nature and destiny." He believed that, if the child has not been warped in its earliest development by allowing its powers to define evil instead of good in its nature, through failure to provide appropriate conditions for its best spiritual growth, it will need no promise of reward to lead it to do right, because, if properly trained, it will enjoy doing right better than wrong. He knew, too, that children who are led to do right by promises of reward are forming the habit of doing when bribed, and not the habit of doing right. They will do wrong as readily as right for bribes in manhood if their moral development is arrested by the substitution of rewards instead of the enjoyment and duty of doing right, as the motive to action.

It is a fallacy to suppose, as so many do, that if children can be led to do right by coercion or by hope of reward, they are forming the habit of right-doing. It is the motive and not the action that becomes habitual by repetition in moral training. The habit that is formed by promising rewards to children is the habit of bribe-taking. Such training makes it impossible to develop the sense of duty and responsibility as the basis for right action. It will help educators to avoid many mistakes if they remember that the originating power is more important than the operative power in the formation of moral habits. Moral habits are the result of moral actions. It is undoubtedly as true in ethical training as in any other department of training that "practice makes perfect," or that repeated action defines power; but it must never be forgotten in any department of training that it is *self*-activity and not mere activity that is truly developing. The selfhood is the originating power, and the formation of moral habits must produce a change in the selfhood. The change wrought by promising rewards or by coercion is weakening. In the first case it is degrading; in the second, it is paralyzing. All external incentives to duty weaken the child's inner self-active motive power, and thus prevent its highest ethical development.

Froebel objected in all training to dogmatic teaching beyond the child's experience. The effects of such teaching in ethical training are even more disastrous than in any other department of training. Vital interest dies when moral and religious theories are given in words before apperceptive centres adapted to the child's stage of development have been formed by experience. The growth must be from the inner to the outer life. There must be some experience to give life and meaning to the words, or they remain dead and meaningless. Confusion results when a child is led to believe that its moral and religious nature is being developed by memorizing statements of theological dogma. Many Christian people only believe they believe. "If a man is to understand religious truth, he must be made to experience much. He must rise gradually to a knowledge of the truths of Christianity." Froebel did not believe it possible to teach temperance, or citizenship, or virtue, or religion from books alone, but held that a good character is developed by good living. Good habits and loving service are better than any formal ethical training. Form and life must be in harmony. Unless dogmatic creeds are illustrated by true lives in those by whom the child's daily life is surrounded, there is great danger that the creeds will be discarded because misunderstood, and that with the creeds will be swept away the child's desire for a higher spiritual life.

Froebel protested against all efforts to force on a child the practice or creed of adults in religious life or profession. He objected to formal religious exercises in schools unless they are adapted to the child's stage of development. He desired that every human being should have his religious feelings developed and applied in childhood. His ideal of the perfect training of a child was to bring it under "the influence of Nature, useful handiwork, and *religious feelings*," but he dreaded nothing more than that the child should become a formalist or a hypocrite. It usually becomes both if adult religion is forced on it prematurely; and formalism and hypocrisy are the most effective agents in destroying the divinity in humanity and in robbing men of true motives. George McDonald describes the process of religious training too often adopted as an attempt to "sandpaper a child into a saint." Religious life must be the result of the out-working of the good feeling and thought of the child's inner life.

The child may be dwarfed religiously either by losing the proper religious culture of the emotions and the senses adapted to the earliest stage in its religious evolution, or by compelling it to assume in childhood the religious life of a later stage of its development.

In his kindergarten and in his directions for mothers he tried to guide the kindergartner or mother to lead the child by her enlightened love through the circumstances and conditions that define and strengthen the principles of sound morality by calling them into practice, and give it such experiences as will lead to the natural unfolding of its religious character, and lay the foundation for a clear, strong, true, and ever-developing spiritual nature. "The boy's life," he says, "should be a prayer of Jesus expressed in conduct and in deeds."

Froebel believed in a thoroughly practical religion. He did not undervalue spirituality, but he saw that religion was too often mere sentiment, a temporary awakening of feeling. He placed a very high value on spirituality, and he therefore desired to weave pure feeling and thought into character by the child's active use of them in its daily life.

He demanded works, not only to show faith but to increase faith. He saw the folly of training a race to believe, or rather to believe they believe, without doing good deeds in accordance with their most enlightened beliefs. "Religion is union with God, and man can be united with God only by seeing, believing, and acting with God, and not by any one of these things alone." Herbart taught that instruction is the chief element in the formation of character. This Froebel did not believe. He substituted creative doing of the right for instruction. Instruction is needed; but neither feeling nor instructed thought becomes a part of a child's nature truly till it is applied by the child in executing a good impulse or plan of its own. Froebel taught that "the worship of God is only one-sided, is only *a temporary social edification*, which deserves not the name of worship if it proves fruitless for the inward and outward life of man." His all-enlightening law of unity made it impossible for him to divorce the spiritual from the practical. Religious feelings and thoughts fade out of life unless they are made a part of life. "Religion is not an emotion or a dogma, but a service."

In all Froebel's teaching, as well as in his organized system of education, he guided the child's work so that its chief joy should be found in rendering service to others who needed it. He knew that the child might be made intensely selfish by making it conscious of its own individual power without at the same time training it to use its powers for others whom it can aid to greater happiness. He gave childhood full opportunity to learn by experience that it is "more blessed to give than to receive"—a truth no one ever understood if he had to learn it by words alone. The child in the kindergarten produces gifts for mother, father, grandparents, sisters, or brothers. They are the results of its creative and constructive power, expressions of its inner life, and, if they are received with joyous appreciation, the child is truly blest by immediate happiness and by unselfish character development. Froebel taught that the true Christmas tree for the child is the tree on which hang gifts made by the child for others. Too often children are made selfish at the time when of all the days in the year they should be trained to understand the joy of giving. Giving to others the results of its own labour foreshadows the nobler duty of self-sacrifice for others who sorrow—a virtue that Froebel aimed to implant in every heart as a golden link to bind the brotherhood of man.

He had little respect for any religion that made the saving of his own soul the supreme end of a man's religious life. He aimed to make men free, that they might develop their selfhood or their inner divinity to its highest limit, but with freedom he always associates responsibility.

Each individual should recognise two dominant duties: First, to bring himself into harmony with universal law, that his own evolution may be complete; second, to become an essential part of the interdependent organic unity of humanity. The recognition of individuality alone may make men selfish, and therefore essentially evil; the training of individual power in order to become a stronger element in the universal brotherhood makes a man at once humble, self-reverent, unselfish, and creatively co-operative.

The Church, by directing the man's attention too exclusively to the salvation of his own soul, was using the highest external moulding agency to make him selfish, and to make atomism or separatism or unrelated individualism the supreme law of humanity. Froebel took direct issue with the Church, and claimed that it grievously misrepresented Christ's teaching. He saw in Christ's revelation to man more than all else the true conception of an interdependent humanity whose inner connection is the Divine element in its nature, and whose destiny is complete unity with God. To make this unity between humanity and God perfect each individual in humanity must establish the unity between himself and God. This Froebel made his highest privilege, because thereby he was doing his most perfect work for humanity and God. Perfect happiness is only possible when man is performing up to his fullest power the best he is now capable of as a step toward the fulfilment of his highest destiny. To guide him in doing this through life is the work of religion. To fit him for it is the aim of ethical training.

Man's highest destiny, according to Froebel, is unity with God. He says: "Religion is the endeavour to raise into clear knowledge the feeling that originally the spiritual self of man is one with God, to realize the unity with God which is founded on this clear knowledge, and to continue to live in this unity with God, serene and strong, in every condition and relation of life." To make this unity possible is the all-pervading, all-inclusive aim of his educational system. In the earlier stages of the child's evolution in the home, the kindergarten, and the primary school, he would implant the germs of unity with God by leading it to recognise the element of life in Nature as the basis of its later recognition of God as the source of life and as the life itself. In the higher departments of the public schools the phenomena of Nature should reveal the laws as well as the life of God, and in the college and university he would make the conception of unity conscious, and develop it as the broad foundation on which to rest all efforts for the amelioration of evil and the development of good. He would make a radical change in the work of colleges and universities by making it chiefly constructive instead of cumulative, so that all the learning and training of the previous stages of educational growth might be co-ordinated and wrought into uplifting, life-impelling forces. All the training of sensations and emotions, and all the acquisition of knowledge, is preparatory to the development of an enlightened, a strong, and a persistent will to make man a self-active power for good.

The conception of perfect unity between individual

man and God is but the basis on which rests the greater unity between God and humanity. The wider ideal is the source of progressive religious growth, according to Froebel's general principle, that the all-inclusive ideal in every department of intellectual and spiritual development is most productive of active, persistent interest and of creative self-activity, and therefore of true growth. He says: "Unless man ascends from the knowledge of the fatherhood of God in his own life to a knowledge of his fatherhood in the life of mankind, future religious instruction will be empty and barren."

Froebel taught the importance of revealing to conscious youth the superiority of the internal when compared with the external, and the fallacy of resting happiness on the variable conditions of outer life, instead of finding its chief joy in "inner freedom, serenity, and contentment." By the true culture of man's spiritual nature he hoped to ennoble him so that he would become free from the aggravating restrictions of material conditions, and use even difficulties and disappointments as elements in his spiritual evolution. "Renunciation," he says, "the abandonment of the external for the sake of securing the internal, is the condition for attaining highest development."

Humanity has been dwarfed by servility to materialism. To remedy this one-sided Christians have attempted to elevate man by a too exclusive spirituality. Froebel aimed to preserve the proper relationship between the two. He made the spiritual the dominant force to utilize material things for high purposes, and thereby hoped ultimately to free man from the slavery of lower desires.

How the race would leap toward the light if it had learned to subordinate the external to the internal!

Froebel aimed to ennoble work—to make it the achievement of creative power, the accomplishment of duty, and the expression of the divinity in man. Work that degenerates into drudgery is a dreadful perversion of high powers. The power to work enables men to prove their love by deeds, and makes a man worthy of his place as an individual in the unity of humanity. Work is a source of development to man's physical, intellectual, and spiritual nature, and it is therefore an important element in ethical culture. It gives a man executive power, and religious life needs the characteristic of achievement. To arouse good feelings without action in response to their promptings is certain to weaken a child's moral force. Froebel believed that all men should be workers, and that working together they would become workers with God.

Mr. Bowen has described Froebel's religious teachings as "the pure, simple view of the Gospels—brotherly kindness, growing up into love of God—living, moving, and having its being in the practice of love. It is a growing into union with humanity and with God by a willing, conscious endeavour to *live out* on earth God's grand purpose in humanity—a purpose which more than once has been made to seem narrow and unattractive, but which, as Froebel expounds it, is again worthy of man and of man's Creator." "This growth, too," he adds, "Froebel's plan is well fitted to produce."

Froebel believed that humanity may develop progressively toward the Divine in conformity with the universal law of evolution; that every child has in its nature an element of divinity which should be fostered and brought into conscious unity with the Divine; that the natural tendency of childhood is toward the right if supplied with right conditions for the growth of its best; that the ideal side of the child's nature should be developed from the moment the baby receives its first impressions to prevent the growth of the sensual in its character; that training should begin at birth, but that it never should interfere with the child's spontaneity; that freedom is the only true condition of perfect growth; that coercion dwarfs and reward-giving as an inducement to good conduct degrades; that positivity or spiritual propulsion is an important element in character; that ethical culture must be given in each stage of development in order that the true growth of succeeding stages may be attained; that it is a grave error to attempt to give the child in any stage of its development ethical training or rules of conduct belonging rightfully to a later stage; that the first germs of religious growth are found in community, love, reverence, filial and fraternal relationships, and true living as revealed by the experiences of pure family life; that Nature is the child's symbolic revealer of God as life in advancing evolution to higher life; that the evil in a child's action results from suppressed or misdirected good; that religion should not be associated with terrors of any kind; that the child's religious experiences should be joyous and happy; that God should be revealed as a loving father; that the child should not be made conscious of evil in its own motives in its early life; that the child's life should be kept free from formalism and hypocrisy; that no dogmatic theology should be given in words until the child has experiences that can give life and meaning to the words; that the child's mind should not be filled with meaningless maxims, mere ashes of dead virtues; that selfhood is the child's divinity and its development the great function of the home and the school; that selfhood should be made complete as a basis for the perfect unity with God and humanity; that self-activity is the process of growth morally as well as intellectually; that right-doing not only demonstrates faith but increases it; and that religion can not be communicated to or taken into the life of man as a completed thing, or by the intellectual acceptance of opinions or doctrines, but that it must be a progressive growth in feeling and thought in which community, love, life, law, reverence, gratitude, joyousness, renunciation, unselfishness, freedom, and creative activity are essential elments.

At first, theologians feared that Froebel was unorthodox, but to-day the most progressive religious leaders are earnestly advocating the vital truths he taught. His insight into the inner meaning of Christ's teaching was truly remarkable. The religious world owes him a deep debt of gratitude for many interpretations of Christ's wonderful lessons, perhaps for none more than for the inspiring revelation that Christ came not alone that men might have life, but that they might have it "more abundantly."

When Froebel's ethical teaching has wrought its perfect work in the homes, the schools, and the churches, then his complete ideal, which is the Gospel ideal in practice, will be the greatest controlling and uplifting force in the world.

INDEX.

THE END.

20 **Rousseau's Émile; or, Treatise on Education.** Translated and annotated by W. H. Payne, Ph. D., LL. D. $1.50.

21. **The Moral Instruction of Children.** By Felix Adler. $1.50.

22. **English Education in the Elementary and Secondary Schools.** By Isaac Sharpless, LL. D., President of Haverford College. $1.00.

23. **Education from a National Standpoint.** By Alfred Fouillée. $1.50.

24. **Mental Development of the Child.** By W. Preyer, Professor of Physiology in Jena. Translated by H. W. Brown. $1.00.

25. **How to Study and Teach History.** By B. A. Hinsdale, Ph. D., LL. D., University of Michigan. $1.50.

26. **Symbolic Education.** A Commentary on Froebel's "Mother-Play." By Susan E. Blow. $1.50.

27 **Systematic Science Teaching.** By Edward Gardnier Howe. $1.50.

28. **The Education of the Greek People.** By Thomas Davidson. $1.50.

29. **The Evolution of the Massachusetts Public-School System.** By G. H. Martin, A. M. $1.50.

30. **Pedagogics of the Kindergarten.** By Friedrich Froebel. $1.50.

31. **The Mottoes and Commentaries of Friedrich Froebel's Mother-Play.** By Susan E. Blow and Henrietta R. Eliot. $1.50.

32. **The Songs and Music of Froebel's Mother-Play.** By Susan E. Blow. $1.50.

33. **The Psychology of Number.** By James A. McLellan, A. M., and John Dewey, Ph. D. $1.50.

34. **Teaching the Language-Arts.** By B. A. Hinsdale, LL. D. $1.00.

35. **The Intellectual and Moral Development of the Child.** Part I. By Gabriel Compayré. Translated by Mary E. Wilson. $1.50.

36. **Herbart's A B C of Sense-Perception, and Introductory Works.** By William J. Eckoff, Pd. D., Ph. D. $1.50.

37. **Psychologic Foundations of Education.** By William T. Harris, A. M., LL. D. $1.50.

38. **The School System of Ontario.** By the Hon. George W. Ross, LL. D., Minister of Education for the Province of Ontario. $1.00.

39. **Principles and Practice of Teaching.** By James Johonnot. $1.50.

40. **School Management and Methods.** By Joseph Baldwin. $1.50.

41. **Froebel's Educational Laws for all Teachers.** By James L. Hughes, Inspector of Schools, Toronto. $1.50.

42. **Bibliography of Education.** By Will S. Monroe, A. B. $2.00.

43. **The Study of the Child.** By A. R. Taylor, Ph. D. $1.50.

44. **Education by Development.** By Friedrich Froebel. Translated by Josephine Jarvis. $1.50.

45. **Letters to a Mother.** By Susan E. Blow. $1.50.

46. **Montaigne's The Education of Children.** Translated by L. E. Rector, Ph. D. $1.00.

47. **The Secondary School System of Germany.** By Frederick E. Bolton. $1.50.

48. **Advanced Elementary Science.** By Edward G. Howe. $1.50.

49. **Dickens as an Educator.** By James L. Hughes. $1.50.

50 **Principles of Education Practically Applied.** By James M. Greenwood. Revised. $1.00.

51. **Student Life and Customs.** By Henry D. Sheldon, Ph.D. $1.20 net.

52. **An Ideal School.** By Preston W. Search. $1.20 net.

53. **Later Infancy of the Child.** By Gabriel Compayré. Translated by Mary E. Wilson. Part II of Vol. 35. $1.20 net.

54. **The Educational Foundations of Trade and Industry.** By Fabian Ware. $1.20 net.
55. **Genetic Psychology for Teachers.** By Charles H. Judd, Ph.D. $1.20 net.
56. **The Evolution of the Elementary Schools of Great Britain.** By James C. Greenough, A.M., LL.D. $1.20 net.
57. **Thomas Platter and the Educational Renaissance of the Sixteenth Century.** By Paul Monroe. $1.20 net.
58. **Educational Issues in the Kindergarten.** By Susan E. Blow. $1.50 net.

OTHER VOLUMES IN PREPARATION.

D. APPLETON AND COMPANY, NEW YORK.